GIVING THE GIFT 🎁 OF PUBLIC SPEAKING

Vince,
You're the best.
Thanks for all you do.
Anne
:)

Giving the Gift of Public Speaking. First Edition
Copyright © 2015 by Anna Echols

All rights reserved. No part of this book may be reproduced in any form whatsoever, by photography, xerography or by any other means, by broadcast or transmission, by translation into any kind of language, nor by recording electronically or otherwise, without permission in writing from the publisher, except by a reviewer, who may quote brief passages in critical articles or reviews.

ISBN 9780993763519

Editorial Assistance by Cori Brownlee, Prairie Girl Editing,
Saint John, NB, Canada

Printed in Canada
by Printorium Bookworks / Island Blue Print Co. Ltd.
Victoria BC

GoodToGreat Public Speaking Training
Tel. 250-217-1811

GIVING THE GIFT 🎁 OF PUBLIC SPEAKING

A Comprehensive Guide to Overcoming Presentation Anxiety

Anna Coleshaw-Echols

Espresso Book Machine
uvic bookstore
SELF-PUBLISHING AND PRINT-ON-DEMAND

Quotes from Clients

"I use the G2G Secret Formula for creating all my speeches now. It takes me less time to craft the speech, and it also makes it easier to deliver my content without notes!"
– Angela Mondor, GeekyGirl.ca

"You will want to read this book for all Anna's secrets of how to make speaking so easy and fun. These easy to use steps, which I have used personally, have assisted me in becoming much more comfortable in front of a room full of eyeballs."
– Lynn Lindberg, A Healthier Way to Live Inc.

"I've used the book to prepare for presentations, meetings and sometimes gatherings of a more social nature. It helps me to get my point across in a way that's organized and easier for others to understand. It has given me the confidence to share ideas and thoughts with people in groups of any size."
– Denis Robidoux, Marymound Inc.

"This easy to follow book is a great tool for those who wish to go from good to great in their public speaking achievements. It really is a gift. There is a "secret formula" that will make all your speeches, presentations and talks SO much easier to plan and give."
- Cheron Long-Landes, Holistic Practitioner

"Anna creates a comfortable way to learn public speaking in this book. She gives helpful tips for everyone to become successful in their speaking techniques. Take a chance and enjoy the experience!"

— Kaydee Deremiens, Sunrise Credit Union

"Anna's book is a wealth of practical information that will give you the edge to become a spectacular speaker. Simple to follow and easy to implement with a touch of heart to inspire you."

— Sheila Dancho, USANA Million Dollar Club member

Contents

Foreword	8
Introduction	10
Is This Book For Me?	12
Dedication	14
How to Best Use this Book	15
Will You Accept My Challenge?	17
A Bit About the Fear of Public Speaking	19
You Are Not Alone	22

SECTION ONE

1 Streamlining the Speech Creation Process	30
2 Topics Discovery	34
3 The Power of Mind Mapping	39

SECTION TWO

The 3T Strategy	44
4 Crafting a Superb Introduction	48
5 Building the Body of Your Presentation	57
6 Concluding Your Presentation	64

SECTION THREE

7 Nine Ways to Keep the Conversation Flowing	72
8 Persuading An Audience	80
9 A Prescription for Ideal Body Language	92
10 Becoming a More Creative Speaker	101

11	Debunking the Practice Makes Perfect Myth	123
12	Ummmm, Eliminating Thinking Noises	136
13	Speech Evaluation Strategies	145
14	Wrapping the Gift With a Bow	155

Appendix A:
G2G Secret Formula Speech Crafting Outline — 159

Appendix B:
General Speech Outline Worksheet — 162

Appendix C:
Speaking Math Calculations — 165

Appendix D:
Questions for Future Speaking Engagements — 167

Acknowledgements — 168

About the Author — 171

Foreword

If you can believe it, each and every one of my school report cards K-grade 12 stated, "Barbara talks too much." Since then, I have taken my "talking too much" to the next level. Today, I am speaker, trainer, author, newspaper columnist, radio host, and book coach. Communicating is my life -- it's my bread and butter.

However, I always keep in mind the old saying, "it's not what you say, but what people hear." In other words, communication doesn't simply mean putting words and thoughts together. It means developing a plan, choosing your words and phrases, and developing your content in the right order. It means researching your audience and selecting the right images so that people can connect with your voice and words. Easy right? No, as a matter of fact it is not easy.

As you may know, there are plenty of books on speech writing, preparing presentations, and speaking to an audience. However, it is rare to find such an easy to follow a book such as Giving the Gift of Public Speaking, written by speaking coach and expert,

Anna Coleshaw-Echols, also known as the "chief fear slayer." It is also rare to find such a talented young author who can translate the tough and fearful subject of speaking into a practical, down to earth guidebook. Anna's "fill in the blanks" approach is so easy; you'll soon master any fear you ever had about speaking.

And that's why this book will be a valuable resource for you. Take a stand. Take action and transform your fear and become fearless forever.

Barbara Bowes, FCHRP, CMC, M.Ed., CCP

President - Certified Coach Practitioner – Professional Speaker
Legacy Bowes Group
www.BarbaraBowes.com

Author of:

- *The Easy Résumé Book: A Transferable Skills Approach*
- *Working World: Employer Guide (vol. 1)*
- *Working World: Employee Guide (vol. 2)*
- *Résumé Rescue: Essential Résumé Saving Techniques*
- *Taming the Workplace Tigers: Powering Your Career to a Roaring Success*
- *Cracking the People Code*

Introduction

Express yourself!

You have something to say. I know you do. Everyone does. Whatever your age, education, lifestyle, everyone is unique and sees the world in a unique way. I know you have something to say. I want to hear it. I want to hear YOU say it. This book will help.

I have known Anna for many years, since we were just little girls starting school, and as her friend and editor I see her passion for helping people share their stories. She genuinely wants to help YOU to share whatever you want to share. Maybe it's a story at a family get together, wedding or even funeral. Maybe you are in school and want to improve your English mark. Maybe you need to present information at a seminar or even just at a booth in the mall. Whatever the opportunity, Anna can help you to polish your presentation skills.

Public speaking is NOT just for the professionals. Everyone, everyday, imparts information to someone, somewhere: teachers, parents, bankers, friends, and students, even just around the dinner table. Communication is a huge part of our lives. Why not take this opportunity to improve your communication skills?

This book is full of great tips and strategies that you can incorporate right now, today. I suggest you take one of Anna's courses if you can, but if you can't, then this book is a great way to begin. I know my own presentation and verbalization skills have improved just through my time spent editing.

Anna's book would also make a great graduation gift. As our children head out into the world, they need the ability to be able to communicate their knowledge and skills. This world is becoming more and more competitive, and the effective communicator will stand out in the crowd.

Go ahead. Take a chance. Express yourself.

Cori Brownlee

Prairie Girl Editing
www.PrairieGirlEditing.com

Is This Book For Me?

Ask yourself these questions...

- ☐ Do you have opportunities to speak on topics that are worthwhile?
- ☐ Does your job require you to present regularly?
- ☐ Do you foresee the need to speak to a group in the next month?
- ☐ Do you have a fear (even a little bit) of speaking in front of a group?
- ☐ Do you have a story to tell, but you're not sure how to organize your words?

If you answered yes to one or more of these questions, then this book may be what you are seeking.

Now consider...

- [ ] If you were asked to speak at an event (of any size) would you accept the opportunity?
- [ ] After a presentation, do you come home invigorated and full of energy?
- [ ] Are you at peace with your public persona when presenting?
- [ ] Are you spending enough time in your life on your own self-development journey?
- [ ] Are you satisfied with the contribution you have made to the world?

If you answered no to even one of these questions, then this book is definitely for you!

Dedication

I dedicate this book to all those in the world who fear public speaking or who possess presentation anxieties and have set themselves a goal to overcome their speaking inhibitions.

It is my honest hope that, after reading this book, you will once and for all be able to conquer your fears and present confidently no matter where you are, and no matter what you are speaking about.

How to Best Use this Book

There is an old joke that's been circulating for years ...

Q: How do you eat an elephant?
A: One bite at a time!

The same is true of changing your approach to public speaking. In my opinion, there is no quick fix or overnight solution -- at least none that I, nor my hundreds of clients, have found. Like everything in life... you get out of an experience what you put into it. As a result, it will take time to completely make over your existing speaking persona and I'd be honoured to assist you in that journey!

I will walk you through preparing to present two of the most popular speech styles. By following my guidance throughout this book, you will learn how to effectively share your knowledge and persuade others through speech presentations while becoming more efficient in your own speech preparation activities. As an added bonus, I'm also sharing creative ways to enhance your future presentations! After all… who wants to watch yet another boring speech? Not me!

Until now, this information has only been available as part of a six-week course called Giving the Gift of Public Speaking that I personally deliver. In these courses, I cram a year or more of public speaking training into a dynamic and fun 36-hour workshop while providing numerous participant opportunities. It's amazing how far my clients can grow in just 42 days, and for those who take my more intensive three and five-day courses, the change is dramatic.

Now that I've condensed the information into this easy to consume book, I'd love to hear your feedback. Please email me at Anna@GoodToGreatPS.com if you have any comments or suggestions. My personal motto is "always be growing!"

Will You Accept My Challenge?

I encourage you to linger and "chew on" on the lessons. My challenge to you is to present these two speech styles to a small group of people you trust. Use their suggestions and review a video recording of your performance(s) to continue on the journey.

After you've finished reading this book I offer a 50% discount a one-hour coaching session (via Skype or FaceTime) for me to view and comment on your speaking persona. You can choose to run through your polished presentation live, or to provide a video to me to evaluate using the criteria in Chapter 13 of this book. I love seeing my recommended strategies in action!

After reading the title of this book you might wonder, "What gift are you giving me?" The tips and strategies in this book are my gift to you, and I hope they inspire you to share your gifts with the world. It is also my hope that you will grow the distance to becoming a very competent and sought-after public speaker. As well, you may find yourself encouraging others around you to conquer their public speaking fears.

Instead of calling myself CEO or President of GoodToGreat Public Speaking Training, I refer to myself as the Chief Fear Slayer. It is my mission in life is to see more people overcome their fear of public speaking.

This book is all about a journey... a journey of discovery where you will find that you too have a proficient public speaker hidden within you. Giving the Gift of Public Speaking is intended to assist beginning speakers to discover their hidden talent by providing useful strategies that can start used right away.

This quote sums up why I teach public speaking and why I have chosen to write this book: to guide my clients and readers in the art of sharing themselves, their experiences, and their life lessons.

> *"When you don't say what you know and feel,*
> *when you withhold yourself, the world is poorer for it."*
> – Lilyan Wilder

What is your own personal motivating quote? Please write it down in a notebook or journal and keep it handy for inspiration and guidance, and reflect on it throughout your journey.

A Bit About the Fear of Public Speaking

I'm so grateful for all I have learned from my clients over the past 16 years. We have so much to share about our life experiences, and there is so much to observe about human nature and how we each conquer our challenges. The public speaking journey is life-long as you can learn something new from every person you meet and every speech you listen to. You may be feeling nervous, worried or afraid. This is common at the beginning of any journey. Use my book as a resource. I am also available to assist you to grow the distance!

No worthwhile journey is complete without your own personal tour guide (me!), so please enjoy the tips, tricks, suggestions, and pointers that I share throughout this book. If you should have a question or two along the way, please feel free to email me at Anna@GoodToGreatPS.com. I'd be happy to answer your burning question at any time.

Picture this… You're sitting nervously in a packed boardroom. You and a group of your co-workers are being asked to share your thoughts about the upcoming changes to the company's daily business practices. This could alternatively be a similar situation at a conference; in a parents group meeting; in a classroom – just about anywhere that you are asked for your opinion or to share your knowledge. However, you are a bit hesitant to speak up and share how the changes will affect the day-to-day activities of your department. What do you do?

Would you like to be one of those people who can clearly articulate their opinions as well as share then eloquently? If so, I can help -- please read on!

Have you ever found yourself in a meeting or gathering and been afraid to share?

Ask yourself these questions…

> Where does the fear come from?
>
> How far back can you track your fear of public speaking?
>
> Is it truly your personal fear?
>
> Is the fear something that you may have learned from someone else in your past?

Fear can be contagious. Like the common cold, people "catch it" from friends, classmates, or family members. We are not taught to be afraid of public speaking; someone shared this fear with you in some way and you learned it from them. It may have been the performance anxiety radiating off your well-meaning mother, sibling, acquaintance or co-worker. Perhaps someone shared his or her story of a presentation gone horribly wrong. Possibly, even someone suggested to you that you should be fearful before you go on stage. If so, it's time for you to let go of this baggage.

If your fears have been learned from another, I'm giving you permission to release your fears of public speaking. To do so simply say to yourself, "return to sender" whenever you feel fear that is not truly your own. I borrow this strategy from the book "Being You. Changing the World. Is Now the Time?" by Dr. Dain Heer, about personal change and shifting perspectives, which I have enjoyed thoroughly.

You Are Not Alone

When asked to state their #1 fear, 40% of people will respond that public speaking is their greatest fear. I have found this to be the true of most people once they find out what I do. Coincidentally, it's the #1 fear of most of my clients!

An exception to this rule was a classroom full of police officers. No, public speaking was not at the top of their lists. Brave souls! Public speaking ranked much lower than their personal safety concerns. BUT... they were still in the class voluntarily to sharpen their presentation skills for professional development. Through my courses, these same men and women go on to wonderfully enhanced careers by mastering their speaking butterflies and learning how to communicate more effectively.

My own personal fear of perfectionism came from wanting to share absolutely everything that I intended to say. Can you relate? If so, I'll share the most valuable public speaking strategy that I have learned thus far -- the audience doesn't know what the audience does not know. Think about it! They've never seen your speech before and they don't have a copy to follow along word for word. So let it go! Let go of the need to be perfectly scripted and memorized, and it will free you to become a much better speaker! With that in mind, I now feel comfortable missing a point or two when I present, as I know that no one will be the wiser.

When identifying the root of our public speaking fear, it's helpful to recall your first public speaking experience. For instance, here is a sidebar about my first brush with my own public speaking fear -- perfectionism...

It was for a school-wide storytelling contest in grade four or five. I won our class competition and was then asked to stand up on a stage and use a microphone in front of a whole gymnasium of my peers and deliver a five-minute "speech." I remember trying to memorize my speech for days and days before my presentation and I recall how hard it was to be "perfect." I wish video cameras had been common at the time, because it would be very interesting to review that tape.

Strangely enough, I actually more vividly recall my rehearsal time in my parents' living room than I do the five or so minutes for which I actually spoke. Thankfully, the speech must have gone well as I have no residual presentation anxiety rooted in that experience. Thinking back on it now, I believe I was afraid of not presenting perfectly, and I vaguely remember going through the knee-knocking stage of nervousness.

What about the fear of forgetting to mention something important? Whether young or old, trying to memorize every word of a speech is quite impossible in most cases. I always knew that I could never make it as an actor as I like to say the same thing in many different ways every time that I present.

Take, for example, the course this book is based on... I have probably presented the course to new clients more than 60 different times over the years. I have my outline, my notes, my PowerPoint slides, my textbook and my pre-written speaking notes. However, each time I taught a class, I thought of a new analogy, or a student asked a new question that took us off on an interesting tangent, and/or I found some new material or read an article the day before class and wanted to share those findings. That's when speaking becomes fun and engaging, even for the speaker!

A speech is meant to be fluid. It's not meant to be constrained by perfection. Being a perfectionist is not a bad thing when it comes to achieving your goals and dreams. But, it can take a lot more time, especially when it comes to memorizing a 20-minute speech. One suggestion I have for you as you read this book is to let your feelings of having to be perfect go. I have noticed that when a speaker is too polished or too exact, they are perceived as more robotic than inspiring.

Let your creativity lead you down the pathway to discovering a new way to present. Let your words flow instead of trying to emulate an actor reading lines. Let yourself be free of a script and apply my fill-in-the-blanks approach to public speaking. You'll save tons of time and stress.

My "Secret Formula" for writing a speech does not involve full sentences or memorization principles. That is really not my style, nor do I enjoy listening to verbatim speakers. Instead, I will teach you how to speak from just a one-page outline, no matter how long your presentation.

Now, take a minute to think about your first memory of giving a speech – jot down your thoughts for later review.

Ask yourself these questions…

>   What did you speak on?
>
>   What do you recall most about the experience?
>
>   What feelings are still associated with that moment?
>
>   How old were you?

Now move forward and consider a time when you felt you didn't present at your best.

Was your speaking time cut short unexpectedly?

Were you unfamiliar with your material?

Was there a heckler in the audience?

Were there any unexpected interruptions or technical failures?

Then ask yourself the following...

What went well?

What didn't go so well?

What would you have done differently?

Now, ask yourself these questions...

Are my past experiences the root cause of my public speaking fear today?

Can I leave those occurrences in the past, treating them as learning experiences and not reasons to continue to be fearful?

If the answer is no, then ask yourself what would it take for you to leave those memories once and for all in the past?

If you are having extreme difficulty in releasing your past, I have clients who have had wonderful success in overcoming subconscious obstacles by using timeline counseling and/or hypnotherapy. I'm not a psychologist, but if your fear is serious, I encourage you to seek out help through your doctor, friends, or family. I find that this quote always helps me to put life into perspective.

> "Yesterday is history. Tomorrow is a mystery.
> Today is a gift. That's why it's called the present."
> - Alice Morse Earle

Just like a sentence, if you also consciously put a "period" at the end of each day and move on the next morning learning from, but not lingering on, your past experiences, then I firmly believe that you will continue to grow the distance each and every day.

After you present, and once you're done and have "come down," as part of your debrief, ask yourself these three probing questions (What went well? What went wrong? What would you do different?) Keep your notes of each presentation in a book called your "Speaking Journal" or in a Word document on your computer. It's simply a place for you to record your observations and to diarize your personal opportunities for growth. Track your progress. Make a few notes of your impressions after each public speaking experience. After a few months, a year, or five years, you'll be amazed by how much you have grown applying the suggestions you will learn in this book. It's all about continuous improvement. Enjoy the journey!

If you are having trouble overcoming your speaking fears, consider purchasing another of my books, Presenting Fearlessly, in which I explore a variety of solutions to the 37 most common presentation anxieties I've encountered. It's a quick read! You can learn more about this book on my website at: www.GoodToGreatPS.com

The path to fearless speaking is simply a series of steps, with each new step building on what has come before. Let's move forward on this journey together, one step at a time – remember that you don't have to eat the whole elephant at once!

As you work through this book you will find that your secret to success begins with being consciously relaxed, utilizing proper breathing, and practicing sufficiently to become comfortable with your material – these three elements are the foundations to becoming a better presenter.

My most important advice is to allot time in your schedule to practice, practice, and practice. In my opinion "winging" a scheduled presentation or speaking off-the-cuff in an unprepared manner only adds to your stress, jangles your nerves, and decreases your effectiveness.

For any presentation, you need to think about what you want to say in advance. For major presentations, you should run through your outline once a day for at least one week prior to your presentation. When possible, schedule a mini presentation to a small group to test your speech before you give it to your main audience. You can also practice silently using the visualization techniques that I share later in this book.

Some experts state that you should practice your speech no more than six times. There is a fine balance between practicing a speech verbatim, saying exactly the same thing over and over again, and a presentation using only the outline approach that I teach in this book. There is a whole section dedicated to exploring practical practice techniques in greater detail in Chapter 11.

Are you ready to start this journey? If so, let's do this together! Anytime you feel like you are getting stuck, or if you would like to clarify some details, you can reach out to me through social media or email. I'm here as your tour guide!

First stop... speaking foundations. After all, a construction crew cannot erect a skyscraper without first preparing the foundation. Let's begin there. Chapter 1 is the foundation for successful presentations.

Seems like you're all set and ready to begin... so here we grow!!!

SECTION ONE

Speaking Foundations

1

Streamlining the Speech Creation Process

I have worked with high school and university students, business owners, professionals and managers, experienced teachers and instructors, and even everyday folk who have a special message to share. I'm constantly surprised by how so many people, even in their 50's and 60's, have never been taught effective public speaking skills. Unless you were in a debate club, or Toastmasters, or had a teacher who had an interest in public speaking, it is likely you were never taught how to properly organize a speech.

Public speaking is an essential skill that is becoming even more important as technology progresses. This makes our lives both harder and easier while creating opportunities we couldn't even dream of a decade ago.

Suddenly, you may find yourself…

- On a video conference call for your small business or a job interview
- Addressing a large community group using PowerPoint

- Giving a national media interview on television or the web
- Recording videos for YouTube viewers around the world

Smartphones, text messaging, and email has created challenges for us as we are encouraged to cease communicating verbally or face to face. When was the last time that you actually talked on the phone to your friends, co-workers or clients? I'm now completely surprised when my phone rings because it rarely does. I do the majority of my work via social media and email. How about you?

Let's not get knee deep into technology… that's a whole book on its own! But if you have a child, niece/nephew or grandchild who's still in school, I encourage you to pick up a copy of this book for them too, so that you can share the experience of learning and take this journey together. Becoming a dynamic verbal communicator will pay huge dividends in the coming decades, and I'd love to see the next generation excel too!

In this chapter, I will share with you the secret to success I've been teaching since 1999. This fill-in-the-blanks speech outline is now called by many clients: Anna's Secret Formula. This outline saves my clients time and energy, and allows them to meet their #1 goal of speaking without notes. After all, who wants to watch another boring note reader deliver a presentation??!

I've already helped hundreds of clients, and my new goal is to share it wider and farther through this book. I would love to see a huge decrease in that 40% fear statistic. If I can contribute to that decrease by teaching my fill-in-the-blanks outline to hundreds of thousands of people, then I'll die a happy lady.

You will learn to skip writing out speeches verbatim. That simply costs you valuable practice time while you edit your pages of material over and over again trying to get your words just right. Words don't matter – delivery does!

The first lesson of speaking success… don't edit a speech with a pen and paper —edit it by doing it, speaking it, and even delivering it over and over again.

Trust me, you will greatly benefits from my secret formula for creating any speech, on any subject, for any occasion. I only ask for your promise… that going forward, you will resist writing your speech out in essay format. Just think about all the time you're going to save!

Example A: Typical Speech Writing Process

1. Develop the speech idea
2. Write like a madman for hours/days
3. Become an editing fiend for hours/days
4. Fine-tune and tweak your "script"
5. Try to memorize the words exactly over and over and over again
6. Practice by speaking it a couple times
7. Skip the live test-run with friends
8. Deliver the speech while fumbling over trying to remember the script
9. Come to the conclusion it was all just a big waste of time and avoid public speaking in the future like the plague

Example B: Anna's Secret Formula

1. Get to the core of your topic
2. Brainstorm the whole topic
3. Pick 3 main points
4. Use the fill-in-the-blanks outline
5. Do an initial verbal run through
6. Tweak the outline
7. Various verbal and non-verbal run throughs with each delivery being unique (not better, just different, is the goal)
8. Test-run with constructive feedback
9. Visualization exercises
10. Video recorded dress rehearsal

11. Final tweak
12. Deliver the speech on the big day
13. Conduct self-critique with or without video
14. Journal for future improvements
15. Repeat this process as often as you can to grow your speaking persona

Though my way may look longer, you will actually take all that time you used to spend writing and editing in Example A and spend it practicing and improving in Example B. Plus, the first four steps of my secret formula can be accomplished in less than one hour for virtually any presentation.

This old adage been around for years: "Tell what you're going to tell them, tell them, and then tell them what you told them." This is actually very apt and applicable for crafting any speech and will serve as our first foundation moving forward – The 3 T's.

My secret formula outline is made up of three parts – a beginning, middle, and an end -- no rocket science here. You already probably knew this tidbit if you've read or studied public speaking at any time in your life. We'll call this the second foundation of speech crafting – Introduction – Body – Conclusion.

2

Topics Discovery

First, you have to know what you're speaking about, and I mean more than just the topic. You need to be a subject matter expert. Keep in mind that this is not school where you were assigned an obscure topic that you knew nothing about. I can assure you that if you stick to what you know, delivering any speech becomes much, much easier and so much less stressful.

On the first day of my Giving the Gift course, I tell participants that they cannot present on a subject that they know nothing about. This is how we used to present in school when our teachers were checking to see what we had learned about the subject matter, and it was just another form of a test. In the real world, and especially in business, rarely are you asked to speak on a subject that you know nothing about.

As we move into the Topic Discovery portion of speech writing, please keep this in mind. If you've never been to the Taj Mahal and have not personally touched its beautiful pink marble, then please do not tell me about the experience. If you've never saved an hour every week using time management principles, then please do not try to teach me how to fix my own time management problems. If you've never persuaded anyone else to buy a new car, nor bought one yourself, then perhaps a different topic would be a better choice for you.

If you have to do more than 10 minutes Internet research then you are either reaching outside the sphere of your knowledge, or you really don't know the subject at all. In my class, the #1 rule for the first presentation is minimal research. No one wants to hear you regurgitate facts. They love hearing stories, especially your stories about how your topic relates to your life! If you go the other route of a "school presentation," it's quite possible that your presentation will just be confusing and you'll be unable to effectively answer any listener questions.

Depending on how many years of education you have completed, you may be more used to the lecture presentation style that your professors and teachers used for decades. They were the experts. They were the ones with all the answers. They did all the talking. It was a one-way push of information. That is not public speaking! Those lecture methods are what we experienced in school but most adult audiences prefer an interactive and informative manner of give and take. Our third foundation is that a presentation is simply a conversation with a group of people. We'll go into more depth on that later.

The Four Considerations

Let's explore potential topics for an informative or demonstration speech, and examine some prospective subjects that have a persuasive component. Keep the following in mind as you begin your preparations.

Consideration 1:
What type of speech do you need to deliver – informative or persuasive? Perhaps a combination of both, time permitting.

Consideration 2:

What is the main goal for your presentation? What do you hope to achieve as an end result?

Consideration 3:

Calculate the Speaking Math using your allotted speaking time. (see Appendix C) This is a determining factor for the width and breadth of information that you will be able to share.

Consideration 4:

Consider the type of occasion, room layout, and all the other variables and constraints. (see Appendix D - Questions for Future Speaking Engagements.) Make a list of the answers because you will need to incorporate those limitations into your presentation.

Each of these steps should be followed for any presentation as certain aspects can limit what and how you are able to share, especially time constraints. There is so much to consider even before you narrow down your topic choice!

Ask yourself these questions...

What do you know about?

List at least ten of your interests, adventures, or skills on the lines below.

_____

_____

_____

_____

_____

It can be difficult to identify what we know. Try this short topic discovery exercise. It will help you to uncover some of the subjects that you could possibly present. Try to think of five to ten subjects for each of the two categories of speeches (info/demo or persuasion) that we will be exploring in the coming pages. Don't limit your topic exploration to just these questions. Use these questions to help brainstorm all the potential topics that you could easily speak about. Finally, don't judge a topic by whether you're an expert, simply brainstorm and write down all potential topics that come to mind while you work through this exercise.

🎁 GIFT TIP: If you get writer's block, call a friend or family member for some assistance. If you want to really stretch your mind... aim for 15 – the more topics, the better!

INFORMATIVE OR DEMONSTRATION SPEECH

This can also be called your "Show Us" speech

Topic examples:

- What lends itself to being shown to a group?
- What are you able to repair at home? At work?
- What knowledge do you have of an object or activity that you could share?
- What strategy or skill are you proficient at?
- What are you always asked to do for/by others?
- What topic is hot right now?

PERSUASIVE OR SELLING SPEECH

In this speech your goal is to change my mind about something

Topic examples:

- Places you've been – restaurants, stores, cities, countries
- Things you've witnessed – events, concerts, musicals, plays, demonstrations

- Experiences you've had – adventures, mishaps, people you've met, goals you've achieved
- Ways to save – time, money, energy, ways to change habits
- What is your #1 pet peeve about people's behaviours?
- What do you really love (or detest) to your core?
- What personal bad habits should we change?
- What would you change in your area of the world?
- What is your favourite cause? charity? belief?

Think of something that you want to change. This is the key to a great persuasive speech. What things you are passionate about? Any topic can be persuasive, but your choice should be of interest to the majority of your audience members.

When selecting social issues, you should consider how open your audience would be to hearing about this topic. Be careful to not pick a topic that is either too obscure or too far out of the realm of possibility of persuading the audience to your viewpoint. Conversely, you also do not want to be "preaching to the choir" with a roomful of believers listening to a subject they know well and about which they are already convinced. More strategies around researching your audience will be included in a Chapter 8.

Even if you've only done something once (like skydiving), it will more than likely make you the expert in the room as not many people have tried a very unique experience such as skydiving. Think of things that you have achieved on your personal bucket list as great potential topics. Next up, we'll start brainstorming to fill the body of your speech by using a unique tool that I fell in love with ages ago.

3

The Power of Mind Mapping

You may have learned this mind mapping brainstorming technique back in your school days, like I did. If not, I'm not going to train you how to mind map, but I highly recommend Googling "how to think like DaVinci" if you're keen to learn more. There are also tons of videos to be found on YouTube if you search for mind mapping. There are some fairly elaborate mind maps out there, but please don't get caught up in the research as I'll show you my own short-cut here.

Spider Web Building

Mind mapping works well for any speech topic and just about anything else in your life too! I love using it for event planning purposes. It's a tool that is well worth learning. I've developed my own mind mapping technique that I like to call "The Spider."

Picture a large web and yourself as a busy Spider filling your web with ideas about your chosen topic. Begin with a mind-dump where you let all your topic ideas and concepts flow onto the paper. This is an excellent exercise for brainstorming in a group, but it works great for solo exploration as well. Some professional speakers even speak right from their Spider when on stage. Talk about cutting down your preparation time!

To start your Spider, ask yourself all the Who-What-Where-When-Why-How type questions that surround your topic. Go around the Spider to create more and more questions that you could answer. Repeat again and again until you are satisfied that you have exhausted your topic. Here's an example for a speech on making homemade salsa. I started by asking myself the "low hanging fruit" type questions that came easily to mind. (See my Spider diagram on the next page.)

Then, I expanded my thoughts by going around the Spider again asking more Who-What-Where-When-Why-How based questions. You are probably able to add at least one or two more layers under each of those questions.

Take your own topic and try this exercise for yourself. Using a blank piece of paper, write your topic or title in the very center of your page. Draw your first Spider "leg" and ask yourself WHO-type questions. Feel free to draw as many offshoots from that one leg that you require as you burrow through all the WHO's of your topic.

Start a second leg and ask yourself WHAT-type questions. Depending on your topic, the first thought you write down may be a definition. If you have chosen an obscure topic that your audience is unfamiliar with, then starting with a definition may be wise. Branch out on the WHAT leg. Do one leg for each of the headings - Who-What-Where-When-Why-How. Then, ask a friend or a family member to help you fill in more blanks.

The key to brainstorming is to let everything flow with no judgment or editing. Get all the spin-off ideas down on paper before you eliminate any. This enables you to unearth as much of the topic as you can. You may find that you need to narrow the topic to just one branch of the Spider, or you may uncover a new path to take for your speech creation.

When you feel you have exhausted the topic then you've reached the end of the Spider Exercise. It may only take 15 minutes, or it may take an hour, depending on how well you know the topic. Remember my rule – speak only of what you know. If you find yourself going off course on a new journey, then simply take out a second piece of paper and start a new Spider and then tuck it away for when you have time to work on it. My social media guru and I like to call these "squirrels" – don't you just hate those pesky distractions too??!

When your brainstorming is completed to your satisfaction, pull out your three main points. You may have to massage the Spider a bit to lump your important points together, but you will be able to find three main points and three sub-points for each main point quite easily.

In life, certain things logically lump together, here are a few examples:

Chronological Lumping:

- Natural Steps to Achieve a Goal
- Stages of Development
- Before – During – After
- Childhood – Young Adult – Adult
- Early Career – Mid Life – Retirement

Categorical Lumping:

- Important aspects of the topic (e.g. 3 considerations)
- Kinds of things or experiences

For as many topics there are in the world, there are as many creative ways to lump them together and create patterns. Once you complete your Spider, you should see the associations and things that will lump themselves nicely together. If not, grab a friend and ask for their assistance for this step. Now, you are ready to begin your speech outline!

This is the foundation of my secret formula for effective speech crafting. Use the Speech Craft Worksheet provided in Appendix A and fill in the blanks to create your speech. This outline has proven to be an awesome tool for hundreds of my clients over the years, and I am sure that it will work for you too. Feel free to adapt it to how you think and process information in order to make it your own.

SECTION TWO

Speech Crafting

The 3T Strategy

"Tell them what you are going to tell them, tell them, and then tell them what you told them."

As you read through this overview of the next three chapters and I expand on my 3T Strategy, keep Appendix A at hand to use as an easy reference for my Secret Formula Speech Crafting Outline.

In public speaking training, this is as old school as it gets, but it's so true. I'm sure you've heard this before, but this is a great tool for building confidence, especially in a beginner.

Keep it as simple as possible, and your listeners will remember what you have said for many years to come.

I always say… "The number one goal of any presentation is to be remembered!" Not for who you are, or what you did during your speech, but for the message that you shared with your audience.

There is a good deal of evidence for the power of the number three...

- North American area codes and telephone prefixes are three numbers
- In Canada, our Postal Codes are two sets of three letters and numbers
- The license plates in North America
- In literature there are often three protagonists, such as the three witches of Macbeth

So why would organizing your speech be any different? Stating three points in your introduction, explaining those three points with three sub-points each in the body of your speech, and restating your three points in your conclusion... brings your listeners back to your key point and increases the power of the number three exponentially in your presentation. Plus it increases the chances that your message will be remembered long-term if you do it right.

Here's an easy strategy for your next speech. When planning your presentation, select three sub-points in such a way that you can take the first letter of each sub-point and make it spell a simple word like C.A.T. or Y.E.S.

The benefit of using a mnemonic device such as this is two-fold. One, it will help you remember the three points of your speech, thus freeing you from the need for notes. Two, it will help your listeners remember your three main points longer. This is especially effective for instructions.

Both outcomes will help to boost your confidence!

If you've ever taken CPR, you may remember the ABC – Airway, Breathing, Circulation. It's been decades since I first took CPR and those three important steps will stick with me always, though I've never had to administer CPR.

For instance, if I was describing the people who live in my former hometown of Winnipeg, I might choose the word C.A.R. and work my sub-points around those letters.

For example, I could talk about how Winnipeggers are very Caring and philanthropic, how they Appreciate summer because winter is long and cold, and how Respectful they are of others, like many Canadians.

And, if I could twist my presentation back around to talking about how when you live in Winnipeg you really need a CAR to get around everywhere because the mass transit options leave a little to be desired... that would add yet another layer of fun into your presentation. However, let's leave speaking outside the box and how to introduce creative platform skills into your presentations until Chapter 10.

CHAPTER 4 – *Crafting a Superb Introduction*

What should happen in the Introduction?

- Set the topic
- Focus on "What's In It For Me?" for the audience
- Apply the first of the 3T's: Tell them what you're going to tell them
- Establish your credibility
- Warm up your audience with a question

CHAPTER 5 – *Building the Body of Your Presentation*

What are the stages within the Body of the speech?
- Apply the second of the 3T's: Tell Them
- State your most important point and support it with your 3 sub points
- State your second point and support it with 3 sub points
- State and support your third point support it with 3 sub points

CHAPTER 6 – *Concluding Your Presentation*

What happens in the Conclusion?

- Apply the final of the 3Ts: Tell Them What You Told Them
- Include a request for or call to action
- Leave your audience with a lasting impression

4

Crafting a Superb Introduction

You may have heard the quote *"Start as you wish to go forward,"* but what does it mean? It means that if you wish to stay strong throughout your presentation, you need to start strong.

I have had clients who build their momentum by easing slowly into their presentation and then ramp up their confidence and energy gradually. However, I prefer to watch a speaker who begins with a strong opening and then continues to build or maintain that high level of energy, enthusiasm, and intensity throughout their presentation. It's much more dynamic and attention-grabbing to start at the higher level of energy. See what works for you but either way, I encourage you to practice your opening remarks so that they are smooth and natural. This will allow you to start strong no matter how jittery you feel.

While there is a lot of information that needs to go into the introduction, the key is to keep it to less than 10% of your total allotted time. Why, you may ask? You want to ensure that you have enough time to expand on the points in the body of your speech as well as adequate time at the end to conduct a proper conclusion. The audience wants you to get to the meat of your presentation, which is what they have come to hear. Give them a teaser in your opening, and then quickly move the heart of your presentation. For a 10-minute speech your introduction should be around 60 seconds, which goes by quicker than you think! This is called "Speaking Math," flip to Appendix C to read more about how to budget your time effective for any speech.

Though brief, the start, or opening, of your presentation is critical to establishing audience interest and setting the stage for what you are going to say. There are many techniques to grab attention, but an essential element is a preview of your main points. In other words, "tell them what you are going to tell them" – the first of the 3T's.

These timing suggestions are not written in stone, but are meant to be guidelines to keep you from lingering too long on either your opening or closing. Depending on the complexity of your topic, you may need to take extra time in your introduction to define your topic. If you're conducting a persuasive presentation, like a charity appeal, you may need a bit more time on the end to tie up all your points into a strong appeal or to ask for support.

What should happen in the Introduction?

Just as I'm taking you on a journey with this book, you are taking your listeners on a journey. Your introduction will let them know what to expect.

1. SET THE TOPIC

There is no better way to grab your audience's attention than with an impactful speech title! You may want to start from the title and work through the outline, or leave the title until the end. I'm about 50/50 when planning my presentations, but I do love working from a wacky speech title as it keeps my energy up through the process. Remember, you're not married to the title, unless someone's given you a specific title to work from, so feel free to experiment a little.

Open your speech by stating the title of your speech aloud, writing it on the board, holding up a sign, opening your PowerPoint presentation with a title page, or whatever creative way you can think of.

If someone else is introducing you, they can state the topic and title on your behalf. However, when I'm presenting, I prefer to provide an introduction that does not give away the topic. It's fun to use a teaser statement that will pique the listener's curiosity.

Pick one of the topics from the previous exercise to work through on the Speech Crafting Outline (Appendix A), and consider "What might be a good title for my speech?"

Example: for a presentation on the how/why of making homemade salsa, an ear-catching title may be "A Journey Through the Flavours of Mexico!" It doesn't give your true topic away, but it grabs the foodie-type people's attention, and it shifts people's mindsets to thoughts of their trips or experiences with Mexico.

Crafting just the right opening title does take skill and creativity. This can be a fun activity to work on with a creative friend, especially if you're feeling stuck.

There are many ways to seize someone's attention. Here are some suggestions…

Use an Engaging Statement

An engaging statement is a means of relating your experiences to the audience to build rapport while grabbing their attention.

Using our salsa example, let's examine some enrolling statements that could be used to open your speech, name your upcoming course, or in any marketing materials you may develop on the subject.

- Save hundreds of dollars on one grocery item
- The secrets of Mexico's #1 condiment
- How to spice up your life!

🎁 GIFT TIP: Think of a couple of different openers for your chosen topic. Test them out on your friends and co-workers to select the best option. If you need assistance, have a look at any continuing education catalogue you may have handy, especially those from your local city's recreation guide. There's some great inspiration all around you, so keep your eyes open for what grabs your attention.

Use Incomplete Sentences

There is nothing that a person craves more than to know what follows…

Yes, I did that on purpose to prove my point. Weren't you curious to know what I was going to write next? Utilizing an incomplete sentence intrigues your listeners. They will want more from you.

As a title headline, this strategy can be compelling, but use it carefully and sparingly i.e. not in every speech you give. Vary the usage of these speech titles each time you present so that you don't get pegged as a dot-dot-dot person. In other words, it's important that you use different strategies for each of your presentations to the same audiences because you may be pigeon-holed as an uncreative speaker who lacks innovation if you use the same techniques over and over again.

Examine your chosen speech topic and design two or three incomplete sentences that you could utilize as a title statement.

Next, test your titles out on a few friends using your Facebook, Twitter or Google+ status posts and see what draws the most attention or click-throughs.

- What I learned yesterday on my course will help me forever to…
- The biggest lesson in life I have learned thus far is…

Curious Statements

Unlike the dot-dot-dot style of titles, the curious statement ends in just one period. You simply want to pique your audience's interest with one strong mind-grabbing sentence. For sensational-style titles, review those tabloid magazine headlines the next time you stand in line at a grocery store cashier. The more startling and unbelievable the title, the better… well, within reason.

Your title must always relate 100% to what you are going to share, to the question you are truly going to answer, or to the solution you will definitely provide in your speech. For instance…

- How leaving my hubby prevented me from overeating
- The one thing I stopped doing that changed my life forever

Now it's your turn -- see how many new titles you can come up with for your upcoming speeches!

_____

_____

_____

_____

_____

2. THE AUDIENCE WILL ALWAYS ASK THEMSELVES
   "What's In It For Me?"

When planning any speech, you should turn your topic around and ask yourself "so what?" "Why do they need to hear this from me?" A good place to start is to determine if you are saving listeners time, money, or energy. Those are great attention getting ways to draw in an audience and have them sitting up straight and leaning into your performance.

As part of the "What's In It For Me?" (W.I.I.F.M.), you should also take what you say to the next level by telling your audience why they should care about your chosen topic. Why should this be important to them right now?

Let's look at our salsa example again:

- Point out how much money they can save. "If you eat a lot of salsa in your household, then this quick recipe could save you big dollars throughout the year!" Maybe have a visual aid or chart handy to show them a comparison.
- If you are presenting this speech right before Cinco de Mayo (May 5th) celebration in Mexico, you could make it topical for anyone considering throwing a big fiesta.
- If you are presenting in January, a popular weight loss month, you may want to showcase how healthy homemade salsa is and how few calories it has, especially when eaten with something other than nacho chips. "So if you're planning to drop a few pounds as your New Years' Resolution, then making your own salsa is a great way to control your calories, salt intake, plus the flavour combinations are unlimited."

3. Tell them what you are going to tell them

The introduction is the teaser, the time to touch on your three key points, but not to expand on them. If we use our salsa example, you may use a sentence like this... "Today I'm going to tell you what ingredients you need to make salsa, show you how to make salsa using your food processor, and then I'll share with you a few of my favourite and more unique salsa variations."

Provide no details and do not expand on those points. You are simply whetting the audience's appetite. After all, the #1 goal of any presentation is to be remembered. You want to grab attention early and keep it right through to the end of your presentation.

By previewing your main points, you help to establish a pattern for listeners to follow. When you tell them you will talk about points A, B, and C, they figuratively label those points as file folders in their minds and wait for you to fill them. As you move from point to point in your presentation, this preview helps your audience follow you with closer attention.

4. Establish your credibility

As I've stressed previously, you cannot present on a subject you know nothing about. In your introduction, you should reassure the audience that you have experience with the topic. If there are "disconnects" between what you say, how you say it, and what your body language shows, then the audience may question your credibility. When the audience does not believe you to be an expert in the subject area on which you are speaking, they will shut down and stop listening. I call this situation the "roll-top shutter effect."

The roll-top shutter effect happens when you…

- Lack expertise and it's evident to your listeners
- Use offensive language
- Present from a point of view that your audience disagrees with
- Don't answer audience questions
- Possess little empathy with their emotions

Can you think of a time when you experienced or witnessed the roll-top shutter effect.

_____

_____

You can establish your credibility yourself, or, if you're lucky enough to be introduced by a formal "emcee," this person can share the details on your behalf. Having someone else introduce you as an expert will enhance your credibility; especially if the emcee or introducer is a highly credible source themselves.

To set your credibility effectively, your goal is to answer these two questions:

1. Why are you an expert on this subject?
2. How much experience do you have with this topic?

Remember, even if you've only done something once, it may be one more time than anyone in your audience – think skydiving.

Let's look at our salsa example again:

> *"I make my own fresh salsa using this method at least twice a month, all year long, and I've been making it for the past nine years."*

5. Warm up your audience

Before you can move on to the Body of your speech, the fun part, you should attempt to get to know your audience. This is a great conversation opportunity. You'll want to involve your listeners in your speech by encouraging their responses from the beginning of your presentation.

There are many ways to do this, but the simplest is to ask a question such as "How many people here have ever made their own salsa?" This gives you an opportunity to identify fellow experts in the room before you assume that you are the only one. For those that answer yes, a follow up question might be "What type of salsa do you make?"

This is called an "icebreaker" or opening statement and can come anytime in your introduction but before you give away your exact speech topic.

These introductory speaking foundations have been tested by hundreds of my clients, and this is one of the best combinations for opening any speech on any topic for any audience – anywhere. The five components of an introduction are in no particular order; so do not feel that this formula is set in stone. When you flip forward to Appendix A to review the outline, feel free to re-order your introduction to fit your personal style and the subject matter you are presenting.

5

Building the Body of Your Presentation

The body of your speech is where you get to have all the fun and spend time (rehearsed time) expanding on what you just teased your audience with in your opening remarks. Now you can "Tell them what you really want to tell them" – the second of the 3T's.

You may have heard of the 80/20 rule in life. This refers to the Pareto Principle. Pareto was an Italian economist who realized that 20% of the population in Italy held 80% of the wealth. Most businesses know that 80% of their business comes from 20% of their customers. No matter how you apply the Pareto Principle, the rule is that 20 percent of something is always responsible for 80 percent of the results.

This principle can even be applied to speech crafting. Again, I refer you to review Appendix C on "Speaking Math." Spending 10% of your time on your introduction and 10% on your conclusion leaves you 80% of allotted time. That 80% can be spent on expanding on your chosen topic. For instance, in a 10-minute presentation, where your introduction and conclusion are 1-minute each, the timing for the body portion of your presentation should be around 8 minutes in length. In a 20-minute presentation, it should be about 16 minutes, give or take, and so on. The example in Appendix C uses a 60-minute presentation for the speaking math calculation.

In the body, you should limit yourself to just three main points. As stated previously, there is tremendous power in the number three, especially when it comes to retention for your listeners. If you're like me, when you run out to the grocery store to pick up a few things, you can easily remember three items but if you have 4 to 7 items, you definitely need to write yourself a list. Sticking to three main points assists the audience's recall, and works to your advantage to help free yourself from the need for copious notes over numerous pages.

Let's use the homemade salsa example again to outline the chosen three main points.

1. Today, I'm going to tell you what ingredients you need to make salsa
2. I'm going to show you how to make salsa using your food processor
3. And then I'll share with you a few of my favourite and more unique salsa variations

It's as easy as that to craft your introduction and then shift those three choices over to the body of your outline to expand upon.

What are the stages within the body of the speech?

If you're feeling overwhelmed or frustrated with deciding what to put into your speech, this section will help you to move forward. The more you use my outline, the easier it will get! By the end of my six-week program, my clients are quite comfortable with this process, as they have utilized this outline to create and deliver four different speeches. Please bear with me and trust in my process. I've seen my secret formula change lives hundreds of times already.

STAGE ONE: Which three main points did you pick for your chosen topic? In the space below, write a one-sentence statement (maximum) for each main point.

1. _____

   _____

2. _____

   _____

3. _____

   _____

If you haven't yet decided which main points to use, return to your Spider and ask yourself which three points would be of most interest to your audience, and/or which three are most topical at this point in time. If you're still having trouble, ask a friend for help. Email me to set up a coaching session anytime you find yourself completely stuck in the development of your presentation.

STAGE TWO: Which of these three points are the most important?

Order your main points 1-2-3. Generally, you will start the body of your speech with your most important point first. There are exceptions to this rule as you'll see when we discuss presenting a persuasive speech.

Look at your points from the audience's perspective. What order would seem logical to them? You may want to test this order with a friend or family member to ensure that it is indeed the most logical order. Your second point will explore the next logical step, and your third point is the least important of the three. This is the same for your sub-points as well.

> 🎁 GIFT TIP: If you do not use your most important point first and chose to use it last, then you must ensure that you have practiced adequately in order to not run out of time before you deliver it.

In our salsa example, the points are laid out in a logical order. You can see how changing those three points around just wouldn't make sense. I could leave the ingredients or recipe to the end, but what would I do if I run out of time? My speech would not be as effective if I didn't tell the audience what it takes to make homemade salsa. It would also not be wise to demonstrate how to make the salsa without introducing the ingredients. You could either introduce the ingredients first or wait to list them as you are describing the method.

STAGE THREE: Building Effective Sub-Points

To decide on the supporting sub-points, return to your Spider to see what details you brainstormed. This is where spending sufficient time on brainstorming can pay huge dividends, as you should have already expanded your thoughts sufficiently on the Spider to allow you to simply pluck your sub-points out. If not, this is a good time to spend another 5 to 10 minutes to expand on the offshoots (or Spider leg hairs) of the main points on your Spider. You should also look around your Spider to determine if any of the other "legs" could be used as sub-points as you may have already completed this step without realizing it. Sometimes using fresh eyes or enlisting a friend's assistance can be helpful in this regard.

For presentations of an hour or more, you may want to restart the Spider process with one Spider for each of the three main points. That should allow you sufficient space on each page in order to expand your thoughts for each point. I have also been known to get out a large sheet of poster board or flipchart paper to give me extra space to "think." This will provide you with additional content to fill the time, and you can utilize the information in Chapter 5 to grow each of your main points using the nine different ways to dialogue with your listeners.

If, when you are practicing your presentation, you find that you are still short on content, simply return to your Spider and look for new points to add or new information to flesh out existing points. These extra points may also be helpful to use as guidance while you are practicing, but you should be able to leave them out of your outline. Most keynote addresses or longer presentations are less than 90 minutes; if your speech is longer than 90 minutes then you're conducting more of a workshop. You can apply the same principles learned here to training sessions by simply treating each half-hour segment as an individual presentation. Use separate fill-in-the-blank outlines for each learning point (training topic). If you'd like assistance with course development, I'd be happy to help guide you, please email me for more details.

Back to your speech crafting… Take a moment to fill in your sub-points below. Again, you should be able to boil down the essence of each sub-point into one sentence or about 5-7 words.

Main Point #1

Sub-point 1A:

Sub-point 1B:

Sub-point 1C:

Main Point #2

Sub-point 2A:

Sub-point 2B:

Sub-point 2C:

Main Point #3

Sub-point 3A:

Sub-point 3B:

Sub-point 3C:

STAGE FOUR: Maintaining your Balance

You want to maintain a balance on the time spent on each of your main points. If you sense an imbalance, then perhaps you need to return to your Spider and select a different combination of points and sub-points. A lopsided speech sits poorly with the audience. They wonder if you're glossing over one point while expanding too much on another point. This is where your "speaking math" comes in. Use this tool to target how long you should spend on each point in order to maintain a sense of time-balance.

Generally, you want each of the three points to have three sub-points. There's that magic of three again! Trust me, if you stick to just three points you will be able to memorize the path of your speech.

In addition, you need to allow opportunity for a bit of conversation throughout your speech. The longer the speech, the smarter it is to build in opportunities for the audience to participate. Be careful not to allow an audience member to monopolize your presentation.

If you're already fretting about how to fill all the time allocated for the sub-points, check out "Keeping the Conversation Flowing" in Chapter 7. It will provide some help with completing your outline in greater detail.

The strategy of ordering points is extremely effective because occasionally your speaking time is cut short at the last minute. This can really throw you off kilter if you don't have a Plan B in your back pocket.

Using the suggested order above, to craft your speech, you can easily eliminate the least important points on your outline. You can either drop your third main point entirely, or simply leave out the third sub-point under each main point in order to save speaking minutes.

Your sub-points are the supporting evidence for each of your main points. These may change depending on your audience. Whether you choose to layout your speech logically as I suggested previously (1st-2nd-3rd), or leave your most important point for last, a 3-2-1 setup, all your explaining is found in the body of your presentation. Once you reach your conclusion, you should be able to "tell them what you told them" without adding any additional points.

Adding more information once you've reached the final minute or two of your presentation only confuses your audience. You can hand out a FAQ Sheet or other type of handout to answer the most frequently asked questions, or you can simply direct your audience to a website to get more details. Ideally, you want to whet your listener's appetites to delve further into your topic. Your goal is to only initiate interest because is no way to address all their concerns, answer all their questions, share every pro or con statement, or to tell them everything about your chosen topic.

6

Concluding Your Presentation

While the conclusion typically comprises less than 10 percent of your total speaking time, it can have the most impact on your audience. The last bit of information your audience hears is typically what they will remember. Carefully consider this question: "What do you want your final impression to be?" This harkens back to the two questions asked in Chapter 2... "What is your main goal for the presentation? What do you hope to achieve as an end result?"

1. Tell them what you told them

There are many techniques that can be used to close a presentation, however, an element that must be included in the closing of any presentation is a summary of your main points. This is where you "tell them what you told them" – the last of the 3Ts. The points review is also the element that many people forget to include.

The magic of "three" works yet again to cement your message in your listener's minds. This will ensure that your speech will be understood and remembered for months, if not years, to come. In your conclusion, recap your three points in the same order you introduced and explained them in the introduction and body.

Many speakers simply finish with what I fondly call a whimper, such as "that concludes my talk," or "that's all I want to cover today." They forget to wrap it up properly. I liken a speech conclusion to wrapping a present, and in this situation, a gift isn't done up properly without placing the final bow on top. There's that darn gift reference again! Please ensure you summarize your keys points in closing. Use those same three sentences that you chose in step one. This will help the audience better remember all that you covered, and it will provide the sense of closure that is required for an effective presentation.

Remember, 10% of your total speaking time is needed to conclude your presentation effectively. There is nothing worse than running out of time. It can be very embarrassing if the time limits are strictly enforced.

For example, I know that in some Toastmasters groups, the audience is trained to start clapping as soon as the red stop light at the timing station indicates your time is over. Practice carefully to ensure that you can cover all the information you have prepared in the time provided. That being said, I always have another point prepared and stuffed in "my rear jeans pocket." That could be an activity or a question that I could ask the group if I find myself running ahead of schedule.

It's important to understand that no matter how much or how effectively you practice your presentation, you will almost always speak just slightly faster (due to nerves) when you present to your audience. If you're presenting and you find yourself a couple minutes ahead of schedule, you can also pull something out of your "back pocket" like a short story or anecdote to fill the extra time.

🎁 GIFT TIP: On your speech outline sheet write Timing Goals. This will help you know where you are spending too much time, or not enough, and if you're watching the clock closes you may be able to use your "back pocket" material.

Suggested timing goals are:

- Finishing your Introduction, especially for longer speeches (45+ minutes)
- Starting Main Point #2
- Finishing Main Point #3 or beginning your Conclusion
- The point at which you ask for questions

In some instances, especially at conferences, you can find yourself stopped by the emcee without being allowed to conclude. Don't let this happen to you. Practice your timing, and watch the clock closely when you're presenting. If you find you've exceeded your goal as you transition from your second main point to your third, then you know that you will have to adjust your final points accordingly to allow the time you planned for your conclusion (i.e. 10% of your total time). If I haven't said it enough… the conclusion is as important, if not more important, than everything else you say – so watch your timing throughout your presentation, not just at the end, when it may be too late to rejig your speech on the fly.

2. CONCLUDE WITH A REQUEST FOR OR CALL TO ACTION

In Chapter 8, we will explore the differences between informative and persuasive presentations, but I'll note here that closing with a call to action is crucial in a persuasive speech. I'm sure you've watched an infomercial and felt the need to call right now to order something – that's exactly how the audience should feel at the end – a need to move forward in some way. It also works very well at the end of any speech but with a softer sell.

For example, if you were demonstrating that homemade salsa recipe as a retailer or entrepreneur, then you would definitely want some jars on hand to sell after your presentation. Or, you could share a taste test with your audience by providing nacho chips and encouraging them to try your recipe.

When you initially crafted your speech, you considered "Why should this be important to the audience now?" and it is in the conclusion where you will reiterate the response. This repetitive tactic is used to strengthen and refresh your listeners' sense of recall. Finally, what can the audience do now to get started? You want to make it "easy to win – hard to lose" (one of my favourite sayings), or in other words, make it simple for your audience to move forward based on your presentation. After all, if they don't take the action step, was it really worth your time to present?

Some examples include...

- How to contact the company or individual
- Where to buy the product or service
- Who to write to in order to take the next step
- What to do as soon as they get home
- What to do first thing tomorrow morning

It is best to make the statement "This is what I want you to do" your very final speaking point in a persuasive presentation: What can you hand out at the end of your speech so that your audience has everything they need to take the first step?

3. Leave a lasting impression

Audiences tend to remember what they hear last. Thus, many presentations end with a question-and-answer (Q&A) session that often deteriorates into a dialogue between the speaker and just a few persistent questioners. In some cases, someone from the audience may make a strong impression on the group that may detract from the message intended by the presenter. The following technique will help you keep control of the Q&A and ensure that you have the last word.

If the situation allows, open the floor to allow your listeners to ask a few questions. However, first state to them that you're also saving the last few minutes of time for your closing remarks. Take questions, keeping a close eye on the clock to reserve time for a proper conclusion. When appropriate, tell the audience you will take one more question, but will be available to answer any additional questions in private after the presentation. Answer the question, and then close strong using my formula. This way, you will have the last word.

When beginning your speech crafting, carefully consider what lasting impression you will leave with your audience. Good choices include any of the following…

- An impactful and relevant quotation
- A jaw-dropping statistic or fact
- A final time or money-saving tip

I have seen some great persuasive speeches. One that stands out and exemplifies this final step was a call to write to government representatives to lend support to an issue. My client had actually written a letter, photocopied it, and included an envelope – one for each member of her audience. All they had to do was sign, seal, and stamp the letter and mail it off to their representative.

Consider how you can take your conclusion to the next level by planning ahead to have handouts to wrap up your presentation. I'll talk more about handouts in Chapter 10, but it's worth mentioning here that I'm a "handout stickler."

Here are my three handout rules…

- A handout should be no more than one page of paper, though it can be double-sided, if you feel the need
- The smaller the better, so just stick to the very relevant facts, as most handouts simply get "round-filed" in the garbage can
- At all costs, avoid white paper as it only gets lost in the shuffle – go for any colour you can, the brighter the better

As shown on the outline in Appendix A, use these three steps in your conclusion. This will set your audience down gently following the journey your speech has led them on.

🎁 GIFT TIP: If you do the conclusion correctly, you may also be able to assist in the transition or segue from your speech to the person who follows you. This can earn bonus points in a corporate or conference setting, and all it takes is a quick question to the next speaker and remembering to jot that detail into your conclusion notes.

And Last But Not Least…

Please, whatever you do, do not end your speech the way Porky Pig does at the end of a Looney Tunes cartoon "That's All Folks!" Never, ever just drop your audience "off a proverbial cliff." It shouldn't be you that says thank you at the end of your presentation. It should be your audience, or at the very least the person who invited you to speak, thanking you for sharing your gift of wisdom!

Putting It All Together

I have heard and remember so many great client presentations because of how well they crafted their speech. It's amazing to think that forevermore when you look at or eat salsa that you will remember me, and what you learned from this book. I'm confident that you are receiving good value and tons of new strategies thus far, but let's wrap up the book in its own "bow" as I have more "gifts" coming up in the next eight chapters.

SECTION THREE

Fine-tuning Your Speaking Persona

7

Nine Ways to Keep the Conversation Flowing

An effective presenter speaks with the audience not just at them. Maintaining a conversation throughout your presentation will sustain audience attention. You will know it's time to spark up some dialogue with your listeners when you notice their interest is lagging.

The longer your speech, the more opportunities you will need to provide your listeners a chance to converse with you. For speeches over 15 minutes in length, try involving them in your speech every 5 to 6 minutes to see if they comprehend what you're sharing.

While you practice breaking the habit of the old-fashioned lecture-style of presenting, here are nine ways to connect with and/or re-engage your audience. Learning to talk with instead of at them will pay huge dividends towards your success as a speaker.

1. ASK A DIRECT QUESTION

You may have experienced the classic schoolteacher move, where he/she asks a question of the kid in the back of the room who is nodding. This is a surprisingly great tool for maintaining interest in adults too.

Use your 5 W's and an H (who, what, where, when, why, & how) to think of some creative questions to get your audience participating in your presentation. There is space on the outline to write them as reminders.

Unlike your more focused opening question, here you can get into the "high-gain" open-ended questions; questions that make the audience pause and contemplate their answers before they respond.

These questions are similar to those high-gain "Miss America" questions that allow contestants to express some of their personality and perspectives…

- How would you…
- What would you do if…
- Why is it important to…

You need to allow time and silence for them to think about and coordinate their personal responses. This isn't a problem when you have time to fill, but if your time is tight, then stick to closed questions that require only a one-word answer or a yes/no response.

🎁 GIFT TIP: After asking a high-gain question, count silently in your head. Force yourself to be silent while you await the first response from your audience. You may even have to bite your tongue to hold back filling the quiet time.

2. Using rhetorical questions

These are questions are asked merely for effect with no answer expected. The answer may be obvious or immediately provided by the questioner.

Rhetorical questions can be effective when used to get the audience thinking along the same lines as you, especially in persuasive speeches, and can be powerful transitions between the points of your presentation.

Some humourous examples of rhetorical questions include:

> *"Marriage is a wonderful institution,*
> *but who would want to live in an institution?"*
> *- H. L. Mencken*

> *"Aren't you glad you use Dial?*
> *Don't you wish everybody did?"*
> *- 1960's TV ad for Dial Soap*

> *"Isn't it a bit unnerving that doctors*
> *call what they do 'practice'?"*
> *- George Carlin*

3. Sharing a story

Occasionally, you may wish to break away from the lectern/podium and "freestyle" by sharing a quick story while you walk around the stage area.

Stories can be real time-eaters so be careful not to wander too far from the path of your speech. A single story woven throughout a speech, especially in longer presentations, is much more effective than one story per main point.

4. Tap your inner movie star

Depending on your topic, you may find wish to invoke your latent acting talent to enhance your speech by re-creating a certain scene in your life – real or fictional. In a speech about spending quality time with the little people in her life, one of my clients re-enacted her young niece's exuberance about her first camping experience and how new, special, and absolutely interesting everything about their campsite was to her.

Re-enacting this scene, was incredibly out of character for this client. She really pushed the envelope that day by adding creativity to her presentation, and it was much appreciated by the audience. It forced her to move about the stage and to raise her arms up high and bend down low, which carried her audience's eyes along with her. This was effective in a long line of presentations and broke up the monotony of staring at a lectern all day.

Re-enacting an experience in the middle of a presentation can be quite shocking to the audience, but if used correctly, you can wake them up and bring the audience along on your ride through time.

5. Visual aids as transitional pieces

Good visual aids and props can add to your comfort level when speaking. It can also elevate your presentation from just a bunch of blah-blah words to something unique and memorable. Audiences love "show and tell," so consider what you can bring along to your presentation to enhance the mood or the audience's comprehension of your topic. It's highly effective – as long as it is related directly to your topic and breaks up the ho-hum of words strung together with something unexpected yet relative.

🎁 GIFT TIP: Hide your prop(s) in a box or behind the lectern. This creates an element of surprise quickly re-engages the audience's eyes and attention. Plus, the anticipation will keep them riveted.

For example, when delivering a speech about a trip to a specific country, various souvenirs (three pieces usually) could be used to transition between the main points. One client used food, art, and regional clothing styles to document her travel, and took the audience along for the journey by showcasing some of the mementos from her trip. This brought the region alive and made us crave those experiences.

6. Be the conductor

Whenever you step up to speak, envision yourself as an orchestra conductor. The conductor has ultimate control over the actions of his musicians. An effective speaker is the same.

Adjusting the tone of your presentation by taking the "reins" and asking the audience to do something – nicely, you will find that most people will listen to you because you're at the front of the "classroom."

Depending on the circumstances you may need to give directions like:

- *"Open your books to page 10"*
- *"Turn to the person beside you and shake their hand and ask them..."*
- *"This is important, you'll want to write this down"*
- *"These are the three most critical steps to succeed at..."*

Remember, as the "conductor," you're in control. So prepare for how you will handle the myriad ways that your listeners can lose attention and focus. If a question or remark is pulling you away from your purpose, then respond with "Let's put that in the parking lot for now and we will come back to it later." or something similar. I've seen this simple statement used to great effect, especially in training sessions, but don't forget to make a note of the query and come back to it as promised at a more appropriate time.

Lastly, an audience can be easily distracted by what's happening outside un-shaded windows, or by what is going on in the hallway; so, don't forget to control your environment accordingly by closing drapes and/or doors. Lead by example and ignore any pesky noises including: car alarms, banging, street noise, or even fire alarms. Remember, if you focus on it, then so will they.

7. Timing your handout distribution

Many presenters will simply hand out their paperwork at the beginning of a presentation, but it can be more effective to share single-page handouts throughout the presentation, and to time their distribution with specific points. People will immediately flip through written material and read ahead of what you are saying. This makes it difficult for them to listen, and it may spoil a big moment that you had planned. Overall it is distracting to everyone.

Worksheets, exercises, or surveys can be handed out at the exact moment you need them for your audience. In a smaller group presentation, this is easily coordinated by giving those sitting on the aisles or edges of tables the correct number of sheets required to supply everyone in that row. Simply arrive early to pre-count and organize your sheets or packages in advance so that you ensure everyone will get one, instead of laying them at each seat ahead of time.

Generally, I prefer to distribute any handouts at the end of a presentation. Keep the handout to one page on which you can provide tips, recipes, a list of do's & don'ts, contact information, or websites for later reference.

8. Making dead air work for you

Most speakers fear pauses and moments of silence, but these can be very effective tools in changing the tone of your presentation, or to regaining the attention of your audience.

Taking a pause from delivering your speech invites comments, questions, and what I call "digestion" of your ideas. These pauses can be easily planned into your speech outline, and if you have trouble with the idea of "hearing crickets" try counting silently in your head to fill the void of sound.

It's a good goal to attempt some silence in each of your speeches. You will find that your audience also appreciates the break in the flow. You can combine such moments with a sip of water before you move on. Simply watch for a perfect opportunity to pause, such as after...

- Stating a statistic
- Showing a complex picture
- Speaking quickly while telling a story

9. Read your audience's body language

While conversing with someone one-on-one, you naturally watch their reactions and check their understanding of what you are discussing by reading their facial expressions. This is also helpful when speaking in front of a group.

Being free from reading your notes allows you to watch for moments of comprehension or confusion on the faces of your audience. You will know when to slow down, or to ask confirming statements of audience members who are displaying visual cues of acceptance (to gain support) or disagreement (watch out for those crossed arms when delivering a persuasive speech). Especially watch for what I call the "Roll-Top Shutter Effect." More on this and body language in Chapter 9.

The actual time slot for your presentation plays a huge role in your listeners' receptivity.

- Some people are not morning people so they're not yet awake
- If it is just before lunch, the stomachs of the participants do their thinking
- Right after lunch, especially a heavy lunch, listeners may doze off
- As the last speaker of the day, you may be competing with their evening plans

Keep all these things in mind while preparing and when analyzing your audience's attentiveness. In these instances, you will need to plan for, and include, more opportunities for interactivity with your audience in order to keep their attention on you and your message.

We've gone through a number of speech creation tips and advice and why these are important to keep in mind. However, when it comes to a presentation with a persuasive or sales-like component there are even more things to consider while crafting a speech. You need to learn about the audience in advance, and to shift your thinking to being completely audience-focused as you develop your presentation. Let's explore how to persuade an audience in greater detail in the next chapter!

8

Persuading An Audience

The goal of a persuasive speech is to change the audience's attitude or behavior. Ask yourself, "What I want the audience to do is…?" In a persuasive speech, you begin with the end in mind. What one Action Step do you want your listeners to take immediately after hearing your speech?

Great persuasive speeches start with an attention-getting opening statement or compelling proposition. By identifying the need or problem that you will address in your speech, you invite the audience to visualize the consequence if that need or problem is not met or solved. You can then suggest solutions to solve the problem or meet the need. Finally, each great persuasive speech closes with a call to action.

Persuading your audience to your point of view is NOT manipulation. It is also not, necessarily, selling the audience something. You do not have to come off as the stereotypical used car salesman to craft a persuasive speech.

When crafting a persuasive speech, consider these three main objectives to develop a complete statement of purpose.

- Provide enough information to create an effective foundation for persuasion.
- Overcome audience resistance or objections, and answer their burning questions.
- Move the listener to a belief or action.

Persuasion skills are useful in many instances including:

- Raising funds for a charity, or non-profit event
- Showing your co-workers an alternate method for achieving results
- Selling yourself in an interview situation
- Speaking on behalf of a group to share or advocate their point of view

Have you had to use persuasive skills in the past? Were you successful at winning over some of your listeners to your point of view? Take a moment to reflect on situations when you have used persuasive speaking, including experiences in your childhood or adolescence. Did you ever have to ask permission to use your parents' vehicle, or for a raise in your allowance? How about arguing for your choice of movie or restaurant? If so, you've used persuasive speech patterns.

What is your #1 pet peeve – the thing that most irritates you when other people do it? This is a perfect example because it does three things...

1. It will get you completely involved in your presentation. Your emotions will be hot and your passions will start to peek out from under that cloak of inhibitions we all wear.
2. When you connect to something that you strongly believe in, which really matters to you, you will be freed from fears of judgment and your presentation style will actually climb to a higher level.

3. You will open yourself to your audience and they will be able to relate to how you think and feel.

When you involve yourself in your presentation, your listeners can better understand your truth, and how you see things. In essence, if you care about something, you get more passionate, have a better presentation, and give your listeners a better idea of who you are.

Move Your Audience to A.C.T.I.O.N.

Before we dive into crafting a persuasive speech/presentation, let's look at the goals of persuasion.

Ask yourself what do you ultimately want your audience to do?

- **A**   Accept your opinions, not agree necessarily with them
- **C**   Care about your cause
- **T**   Take time to reflect on your message
- **I**   Desire to investigate further
- **O**   Form their own opinions
- **N**   Either move away from or towards a NO decision

The structure of a persuasive speech needs to be analyzed differently than an information speech. So, you may want to re-work a few points or shift their order for greater impact. You will also need to research your listeners to a greater degree. For example, if your pet peeve is that males in your household don't put the toilet seat down, what would happen if you arrived and learned you were about to deliver your persuasive speech to a room full of women? You want to carefully consider demographic, socio-economic, and other factors.

Who's Listening?

It is important that you do not view your listeners in an "It or

They" way. As well, avoid making hasty generalizations about your audience, or seeing the audience as a single unit. Instead, view your listeners as individuals. Speak to the audience as unique individuals instead of a faceless mass and you will find that you have much better success at connecting with them.

In preparation for your speech you need to know:

- Who are you talking to?
- What do you want to say to them?
- Why do these people need to hear this right now?
- What do you want them to do?

To ensure your message gets across effectively and as intended, you need to be able to relate to your audience on their terms. If you don't know... ask. There are many ways to determine an audience's viewpoint including in-depth surveys, quick polls, or simply call up a few attendees in advance and ask them. You can also ask the organizer in advance, or simply utilize a conversation within your presentation to unearth answers to the questions below.

Targeting your remarks to your audience's core values is the surest way to ensure that you will achieve your goal. Think about what you know about the audience. Where do they work? Where are they in their lifecycle? Do they have children? Are there any hobbies that the group has in common?

To create an appropriate presentation, you must also consider the audience in terms of their level of knowledge, their degree of formality, and the type of language they use. The Spider technique we used previously can work very effectively here too.

Ask yourself questions like:
Who – What – Where – When – Why – How
in regard to your audience.

- What is the benefit of your presentation to the audience?
- What do members of the audience do? (Are they

students, lecturers, or others?)
- Who do they work for? (If appropriate)
- What do they already know about your subject matter?
- What will be new to them?
- What is the history of the relationship between yourself and the people in the audience? Do they trust you? Will they believe you?
- What interests your audience – are there any subjects that they care passionately about?
- Will anything that you are going to say alarm them?
- What is their educational level? Can you throw 50-cent words around and technical terms galore to a room full of PhD's? Or do you need to take a more "average person" approach?
- What is the background of your audience? What have they experienced? Do they have a common story? Are there things that may offend them due to their racial or cultural background?
- Do they have common concerns or hot buttons?
- Is attendance voluntary, or will you be speaking to a resistant group of people?
- What time of day are you speaking? This is a big factor in how interactive you want to be.
- And perhaps the most important of all… What do they know about you?

You will have trouble if you assume things about your listeners. If you don't know, don't assume.

Once you've considered each of these points, you can begin to tailor your presentation accordingly, using what you know of your audience. Not only will that add to your confidence, but your presentation will be of more interest and benefit to the majority of your audience members.

Again, you should aim to talk with them (conversation) not at them (lecture). You should also build in opportunities to capture greater detail about your listeners, using close-ended questions that will elicit quick yes or no, or show of hands, type responses. For a persuasive speech, conduct research not only of your audience but also of your subject so that you have a firm grasp of relevant facts. But I implore you to not get lost in statistics. One or two statistics, or a couple of strong research facts are enough to support your persuasive argument. You could also use examples from your own experience, or experiences that others have relayed to you.

> 🎁 GIFT TIP: When considering using a statistic, ask yourself "*So What?*" This will lead you to explain the statistic as one key supporting point to your argument. Percentages and big numbers don't translate quickly into people's minds, so always make sure you explain what you are highlighting.

To be most effective, you will need to employ your own logic and reasoning. Test the logic of your speech on a few people or smaller group before you deliver it to a wider audience. Ensure that you have planned your main points effectively and concisely. Sometimes a trial run and/or video recording review will show you where you can slice off minutes by leaving out certain redundant points and/or where a point requires additional explanation.

CRAFTING A PERSUASIVE PLAN

1. *Your Focus*

What is the focus of your speech, and what is your stance on the subject?

Be honest and upfront with your audience on where you stand on your chosen subject. Although I have seen some clients wait until the conclusion of a persuasive speech to tell the audience their personal stance on the subject, this may (and usually does) confuse the audience. My advice is to plan to articulate your position on the topic in the introduction of your speech.

2. *Decision Goal*

What decision do you want your audience to make?
You may elect to wait until your conclusion to state the decision or action you want your listeners to make or take, but I encourage you to plant some sort of seed in your introduction. Doing so will allow your audience to get comfortable with the path on which you are leading them. It's best to set the direction at the outset, but you can leave this for your ending IF you've practiced and tested your presentation well.

3. *Perception Change*

Why should they care or change their perception of the topic?

Your listener's reaction is more important in a persuasive presentation than in any other speech. You want to encourage the audience to sit up and listen. If you can tap into their emotions from the start it will be much easier to speak to your main points. Imagine seeing heads nodding along with you and how encouraging that will be when you maintain an audience-focused demeanor.

To do this most successfully, you need to research the audience. Can you poll them beforehand with a short survey about your topic without giving it away? For example, if you were planning to speak on why everyone should own a dog, you would need to know how many people in the room detested pets, had cats, or even already owned one or more dogs. You may find that your whole topic is problematic and you may need to consider a different topic altogether.

4. *Immediate Relativity*

Why should this topic be important to your audience now?

This question can be especially important if there are any deadlines or reasons that they should take action immediately! It's always most impactful when your topic is current, and immediately relevant. Your presentation can lose impact when there is no immediate requirement of your audience to act now. If you find yourself with that type of topic, then you can creatively tailor your presentation to amp up the need for action now. Explain within your main points what a delay of action could mean (doom and gloom stance) how much more garbage could be built up, how many more people will be hurt. Or the opposite of those (achieving a happy utopia), speak about how much cleaner the river could run now; or how many people could be saved, etc.

Look ahead to what is happening in the next month, or read the news to see what is hitting the headlines that could require a group of people to take action. However, connect the topic to your core beliefs, and don't just pick a topic because it's the latest buzz. You will want to have had experience with the topic.

5. Your Experience

How much experience do you have with this topic?

Establish your credibility early and tell the audience why you are an expert on this subject. Going back to our salsa example, you should know that I have been making the salsa recipe on my food blog (LunchFor1.com) since 2005, probably 30 to 40 preparations. That would qualify me as an expert, right? But even if I'd only made it once, chances are good that that's one more time than anyone else listening – at least for this specific recipe.

Going back again to our skydiving example, I really do not want to hear a persuasive speech on this topic from someone who has never jumped out of an airplane, do I? On the other hand, even if you've only gone skydiving once in your life, you are an expert in my eyes. Pick a topic that you have done at least once.

6. Logical Steps

What are the three most logical steps to convince your audience? Using the Spider technique, carefully review all the main points that you brainstormed for this topic. Getting input from others, especially those with a similar experience level, can be helpful in creating an effective presentation.

Let's take that earlier example of skydiving and follow it through.

Main Point #1:

What is your skydiving experience? Where did you do it? Was it a good experience or a bad experience? Would you go again? This is where you can put your own feelings and experiences into the story as people don't really want to hear a bunch of statistics and such up front, they are already curious to know what it felt like when you went skydiving.

Main Point #2:

Is it safe? When speaking to a room filled with low-adventure newbies, your next logical point may be to talk about safety, and do's and don'ts of picking a reputable skydiving company. Is it fun? But if you're talking to a room full of risk-takers and extreme sporting fans then they may want to hear more about the sights, sounds, and experiences, not to mention see some pictures of how neat your skydiving zone looked from the air as you came down. You would want to inspire those types of folks with tales of excitement and talk about the adrenaline rush.

Main Point #3:

What did it feel like? Here you may want to describe a mental image and walk through your emotional state during the experience. Did you feel a sense of exhilaration or were you scared? Allow your emotions to enter into the speech throughout but heighten your descriptions of your emotions in this portion of your presentation as you build the intensity towards the end.

In your introduction, don't go into detail on any of these points. Simply mention the three main points, which will allow you to expand on them in the body of your speech. Remember, we're just "telling them what we are going to tell them."

7. Identify the Experts

What else you want to know about your audience before you begin?

To create an engaging conversation starter, think carefully about a research question you could use to open your speech. This part of your introduction is a make it or break it opportunity to dig into who your audience is and in what they believe. I cannot stress enough how important research is for a persuasive speech.

What if you were trying to persuade your audience to try skydiving for the first time and found you were speaking to a room full of fellow enthusiasts? What would you do then?

Alternatively, what if you knew that only a couple of people had gone skydiving before? Wouldn't they make great allies to expand on your own experiences? If you knew of their existence prior to the speech, you could use them to solidify your reasoning with the audience by working their stories and experiences into your limited time on stage.

HELPFUL STRATEGIES FOR SUCCESSFUL PERSUASIVE SPEECHES

Do use the F.A.B. Method of stating the features, advantages, benefits of your topic. As they say in advertising… sell the sizzle not the steak. This means that you want to point out your topic's features, but you also want to focus on the advantages and benefits of your topic for your audience. Avoid comparing and contrasting the information because it's a time waster. There is really no need to show the other side of your chosen topic.

Ask yourself why this topic should be important to your listeners.

To be most effective, you need to be able to translate a boring fact (feature) into words that spark the listener's interest and answers the question "So What?" or "What's in it for me?" Benefits to your listeners are more important than advantages, here's an example:

Feature: This car can go 1,000kms on one tank of gas

Advantage: You don't need to fill up as often, maybe only once a month

Benefit: You will save time by not having to stop at the gas station every week

Do remember to clearly state your *"what's in it for me* **(W.I.I.F.M.)" for the audience members**. What is it about your speech that will save the audience time, energy, money, etc.?

Do use follow-up material - Leave the audience with helpful and relevant follow-up material. What is the next step? Provide a brochure, phone number, website, or step-by-step handout, etc.

Do speak to your audience, not your notes - Lengthy notes should really not be necessary for this type of presentation, as they will distract you and the audience from your message. Try to use only a slim outline of the speech. Begin with the example in this chapter and then slim it down to less than one page.

Do aim to have high memorability - Being remembered is the #1 goal of all presentations. How are you going to be remembered? Most speakers simply present a topic and don't think about its long-term impact. How long do you want to be remembered? How are you going to ensure that the audience will remember your message? Creativity plays a role here too!

Memorability is never more important than when giving a persuasive speech. You want the audience to think of your presentation every time one of your key points or your topic is mentioned. You also want them to be able to take action, easily, and to remember what steps to take.

Finally, when it comes to persuading an audience, nothing speaks louder than your body language. In the next chapter, I will expand on a variety of non-verbal communication strategies that will enhance your speaking persona and the effectiveness of your future speech delivery attempts.

9

A Prescription for Ideal Body Language

Understanding the impact of body language is important because much of what you don't say is being said by your physical presentation – how you stand, your posture, what you do with your arms, your facial expressions, and your eye movement. Body language is defined by Dictionary.com as "the process of communicating nonverbally through conscious or unconscious gestures and movements," and it makes up the larger percentage (55%) of your face-to-face communications.

Most people naturally read body language. The most important thing to remember is that your non-verbal signals need to match the words you are speaking. Research has shown that when your non-verbal and verbal signs disagree, people will believe the non-verbal language rather than what you are saying. When what we see is incongruent with what we are hearing, we become confused, concerned, distracted, and perhaps even distrusting. For example…

1. Look at yourself in the mirror and say "yes" enthusiastically, while scowling and vigorously shaking

your head side-to-side "no." Do you believe yourself?

2. Watch a television news reporter's facial expressions closely while they deliver a serious story. Sometimes you will catch them with a slight grin or smirk on their face as they change stories. That incongruent facial expression to the story they are sharing. Does the presenter appear authentic?

Your body language is a valuable visual aid that can help you more clearly convey the key message in any presentation. The best method for analyzing your own body language is to video record each of your presentations (see more in Chapter 11). When you review your video, observe your body language (what your body says) and how it relates to your verbal message (what your mouth says). Make sure that each of your movements has meaning by keeping them linked and relevant to exactly what you are saying. I call this gesture matching.

My Personal Prescription for Ideal Body Language

Try the following exercise. Close your eyes and picture someone whom you believe to be a confident public speaker. What do they look like as they deliver their speech? Not their words, but overall, head-to-toe (H2T) body language? If nothing comes to mind when you review these questions, then open up YouTube and watch a few speeches. If you're still having problems, try watching each speech with the sound muted.

How do they stand?

_____

_____

At what level do they hold their chin?

_____

_____

Are they stuck in one place, or do they move around purposefully?

What are their arms doing?

Do they make eye contact around the room?

How do they move their arms?

Do they make different gestures each time?

Are their gestures smooth and full, or are their arm/hand movements abrupt?

Is the expression on their face pleasing and open, or menacing?

_____

_____

This exercise is a great first step to increasing your awareness of how much body language is contributing to any presentation. Here is my personal prescription for ideal body language for a presenter...

STANCE

Your posture should be poised, confident, comfortable, erect (not leaning), and relaxed. Your shoulders should be square to your hips and relaxed, not up by your ears. Any tightness in your upper body (shoulders and neck) will be reflected in the quality of your voice. This is why full-body relaxation exercises prior to a presentation are helpful.

The majority of your body language should be delivered from your hips up. As for your anchors – your feet -- ensure that you "plant" them in one place while you speak and keep them as still as possible. When you are stationary (not moving with purpose), your feet should be not quite shoulder width apart and pointing towards your audience. You should be equally balanced on both feet.

Keep your chin up at a level position to your chest. It not only shows confidence, but will also assist in proper breathing techniques by keeping your air passageways open. Be careful not to lift your chin too high, as you don't want to appear to be peering down your nose at the audience.

Movement from your hips down should be minimal.

- Leaning with your hip popped out, or leaning on a piece of furniture sends too casual a message in a formal

presentation.
- Standing with one foot tucked behind the other can look off-balanced.
- Dancing or shuffling feet that have no real purpose can be distracting.
- Conducting repetitive (even slight) knee bends, or bobbing, broadcasts your nerves to your audience.
- Swiveling at your hips while addressing the audience on your left or right if not as effective as moving to reposition your feet for a minute or two to address that side of the room.

Movement

Never stand in just one spot to deliver your whole presentation, unless it's for a press conference and the television cameras are trained on you. Your body movements should be fluid, animated, graceful, and purposeful. Move with purpose, around and about your space in order to enhance your listeners' attentiveness.

Movement maintains audience interest by keeping the listeners' eyes following you. Once you move away from centre stage, you should plan to spend at least a couple minutes (more in longer presentations) in one place while speaking. Plan to move every 3 to 5 minutes in a longer speech, or at least a couple times in shorter speeches.

One challenge you need to consciously avoid is looking like a caged tiger pacing back and forth too quickly without pausing to speak. Set yourself up to move from one area to another to showcase a visual aid or to move closer to your audience to make a point.

Be aware of micro-movements or shifting your weight from foot to foot repeatedly. Movement means taking more than three steps, and not simply one step forward and one step backward, or side-to-side. Those little shifts can become annoying to your audience, and they are highly ineffective and serve no purpose.

Gestures

Gestures should be natural, appear spontaneous (not rehearsed), meaningful, lively, expansive, precise, and aimed at enhancing your overall verbal message. When you are not punctuating your speech with an appropriate gesture, your arms should be hanging relaxed at your sides to help you maintain and open and welcoming stance.

Here are four no-no's of gesturing...

- Hands in your pockets -- which inhibits gestures
- Hands glued to the sides of the lectern -- which promotes leaning
- Hands clasped in front of or behind you -- which closes down your posture and makes you look smaller
- Hands on your hips -- which can channel an angry or lecturing schoolteacher or parent

Remember that often you will be presenting behind a lectern, so you must practice bringing your arms up high enough so that the audience can see them. When you're ready to gesture, you'll want to engage your shoulder muscles and bring your arms up to or past shoulder height. Ineffective speakers use only their wrists or elbows to gesture, which hampers the full communication of their nonverbal language. To be most effective, the majority of your hand gestures should occur between your upper chest and your ears.

🎁 GIFT TIP: The bigger the room you are speaking in... the bigger and grander your gestures should be. If you are only using your wrist or elbow muscles, and are gesturing below your waist -- you are totally wasting your energy as no one can see what you're doing.

The best way to improve your gestures is by practice! You can add meaningful gestures by choreographing natural-looking movements into your presentations and by matching your words to your gestures. Try one or two gestures that match up to your words while rehearsing a presentation to get a feel for the movement. You don't want to over-gesture, but you do want your arms to move at least every couple minutes.

For example, if you want to talk about the three challenges your organization is currently facing, practice saying that line while holding up three fingers with your arm slightly raised and extended. Make a slow motion gesture so that it adds some meaning to what you are saying. Practice this a few times until it feels comfortable.

Look for other gestures that can enhance your verbal message. Try to add new gestures to your presentation each time you practice or present and eventually, it will feel natural to create arm movements while you speak. Practice adding in more gestures in your everyday conversations as well.

Eye Contact

Some consultants tell their clients to pretend that the audience is naked. I absolutely disagree with this because…

- (a) Nothing could be further from the truth.
- (b) It will never happen.
- (c) It's embarrassing to look at naked strangers or clients, and it certainly will not help you make better eye contact.

Instead, visualize something positive like nodding heads and your listeners leaning forward in rapt attention to hear everything you have to share.

Making eye contact is only possible by looking up from your notes. This is the #1 way to show your personal confidence on stage. Make contact and sustain a short connection with a few audience members throughout your presentation. Share your connections around the room – from front to back and from left to right – rather than just focusing on one person.

Instead of glancing at the audience or worse, looking over their heads, pretend your eyes are like the electrical plug found on the end of an appliance and "plug into" your audience's eyes. You'll find that two seconds per person is sufficient to let them know that you are really seeing them. Your eye contact should be natural, smooth, varied, in no set pattern, and establish bonds with your listeners similar to a one-on-one conversation.

Facial Expressions

Just as you will practice adding gestures, you need to practice facial expressions. Your facial expressions should be animated, friendly, natural, genuine, and appropriate to your speech content. Remember that TV news reporter example from earlier? You do not want to show a severe countenance when joking with your audience. At the same time, you do not want to be smiling while delivering a grave fact or statistic such as fatality rates or when telling a sad story.

Use a mirror to practice a few facial expressions, but avoid practicing your whole speech in front of a mirror. Instead, choose a few important parts of your presentation that you wish to highlight with enhanced facial expressions, and then check the look on your face while practicing just those sentences in the mirror.

Video-record your practice presentation and watch it at least once with no sound. Watch for all your non-verbal cues, quirks, and contradictory facial expressions. What story is your body telling that you didn't intend to convey? Remember, 55% of your message is being told by your body language.

Ask yourself: *How does my body language contribute to the overall message of my presentation?*

Studying the body language of other speakers and assessing how and what you feel as they present is an excellent way to learn what to do and not do when speaking. YouTube can be a best friend on your journey to improving your personal speaking persona. Check out my ebook, *Avoiding Presentation Pitfalls: Public Speaking Taboos* (available October 2015) where I expand on body language and other strategies in greater detail.

10

Becoming a More Creative Speaker

If your #1 goal is to be remembered... then, one way to definitely do so is to be more creative than other speakers that the audience has seen. This is not about learning a magic trick or doing something to stand out from the crowd. You just don't want to be another talking head at the microphone.

There are many methods to employ creativity, both subtle and grandiose that we will examine throughout this chapter. But first, please keep in mind these statistics.

THE MEMORABILITY QUOTIENT
An audience will only remember...

10% of what they READ
Don't just flash a statistic on the screen

20% of what they HEAR
Have them read/say it aloud

30% of what they SEE
A picture is worth a thousand words

50% of what they SEE & HEAR
Incorporate sound or music into your presentation

70% of what they SAY
Repeat after me

90% of what they SAY as they DO something
Combine multiple senses to score higher memorability!

Reflecting on your past speaking opportunities, what could you have done to increase your Memorability Quotient? Not to harp on it (but I will), if the #1 goal of any presentation is to be remembered, then recall and review your last presentation as you read through this chapter. Make a few notes below on how you could make your topic, message and three points become cemented in the minds of your listeners for months and years to come.

Take a moment right now to write down a few creative self-improvement points.

_____

_____

_____

_____

🎁 GIFT TIP: As part of your speech debrief, use a journal to record your "Aha Moments." Also, include any "Aha Moments" you experience while watching others present in order to grow your own speaking creativity.

- Can you recall a presentation that stands out in your memory?
- Did the speaker use more of the senses, or ask you to recall tastes, scents or sounds?
- Did they make their own experiences come alive by the word pictures they painted?

If you have the time, I highly recommend popping onto YouTube to watch a few TED Talks videos, or other motivational speakers, to see what you can glean from their use of creativity in their presentation. Feel free to record your impressions, likes, and dislikes below.

_____

_____

_____

_____

Being creative not only engages your audience in your presentation but it also engages you in your presentation. It can also decrease your level of fear by giving you something to think about other than the eyeballs watching you. Be careful not to "stretch" your creativity too far. You don't want to appear to be trying too hard, and you do not want to overwhelm the audience with a theatrical style production that is totally over the top.

It's important to look natural while presenting, so use what you innately know to be creative.

Ask yourself these questions…

- What does creativity mean to you?
- How would you define creativity?

- How are you already creative in your everyday life?
- What have you used creativity to make or fix in the past year?

(Hint: creativity sometimes masks itself as resourcefulness)

I recently witnessed a speaker tap into her creativity in a speech by likening the development of her idea for a contest to the growth of a stem of wheat. It was a fascinating example, and I remember being enchanted that she took the time to enhance her presentation with a visual example that so closely matched her presentation goal. She didn't stretch to add it into her speech – it was a very natural enhancement that paid off big time in the audience's reaction to her story.

Creativity and the Five Senses

As showcased in the Memorability Quotient that opened this chapter, an effective way to enhance the creative experience for your audience is to involve all of their senses. Consider ways to link your chosen topic to all five senses. Let's go back to our salsa example…

Sight

- Posters
- Colour
- Pictures

If you don't have photos of Mexico or the southwestern United States, then you probably know someone who does, or you can get them online for your presentation. For high-level presentations, check out stock photo websites for excellent high-resolution photo purchases to enhance your presentation.

When you are using other people's art or photographs, don't forget to give credit where credit is due; a photo credit line in your presentation on the image usually suffices if the image is not copyrighted i.e. royalty free. A word of caution…remember to check the permissions and search for royalty free images or you may find yourself slapped with a hefty invoice.

Smell

- Candles
- Food
- Perfume

If your speech happens to be about food, simply opening your prepared item for most food demonstrations will provide enough of an aroma. However, you might also be able to use candles or room sprays to "scent" the atmosphere. Picture a pine scent wafting through your speech about cutting down your first Christmas tree. Be creative, and paint a "smell picture" for your listeners.

🎁 GIFT TIP: Use caution with scents and be respectful of scent-allergies. It is best to provide a warning for listeners to stay back from the front if they are sensitive to scents. To err on the side of caution, you may want to double check regarding scent sensitivities before planning to use heavy scents or smells in your presentation. There are so many allergies and environmental sensitivities these days that you do not want to cause an allergic or other negative reaction part way through your speech.

Touch

- Props
- Textures
- Tactile descriptions

Depending on what you are presenting, you may want to incorporate props. Going back to our salsa-making example, if you can easily grab a Mexican or Southwestern-style blanket, a poster, or anything else that says "Mexico," you're half-way there.

Dollar stores are a great resource for quick and cheap props. You can bring a souvenir or other prop that can be passed around to a smaller group.

A larger group takes a bit more planning, but it can be done. You may need more samples so that everyone can get their hands on them. Depending on your chosen topic, resources and/or access to willing suppliers, you may be able to afford to purchase sufficient quantities or ask the supplier for a donation of product to showcase during your presentation.

Hearing

- Music
- Video
- Instruments

You can completely transport your audience with music of a region, sounds of a bustling market, or the waves surrounding a seaside resort. Don't limit your sounds to only your presentation; you can be playing music as the audience enters in order to set the mood.

Are you able to play an instrument, or do you know someone who can? If not, enhance your message with a tune by utilizing a CD or MP3 player. Simply singing a little ditty, or an excerpt from a song, can be a great way to enhance a presentation.

Including sound in your presentation can be used effectively to frame your message – oh, can't you just hear the gondoliers singing "O Sole Mio" on the canals of Venice?

In the days prior to your presentation, ensure there is adequate amplification provided within the venue, especially for larger groups. Prior to your presentation, you will need to learn and be comfortable with how to start and stop the sound, as well as control the volume.

🎁 **GIFT TIP:** It's always helpful to ask for an assistant to relieve you of these technical audio-visual duties so that you are free to be the presenter and not the technician.

TASTING

- Food
- Candy
- Liquids
- Foodie-like descriptions

Handling food or drink items can be tricky but, for example, in the case of a salsa making demonstration, you definitely want to provide samples of the finished product, with nacho chips, of course. One of my clients did a presentation on organic apples and brought us two samples, which she cut up so that we could compare the taste for ourselves. All these years later, I still remember this strategy. It was so much more effective than just telling me that organic tasted better.

CREATIVELY ENHANCING YOUR SPEAKING ENVIRONMENT

The following are a couple ways to easily set the stage and control the mood of your speaking environment:

VARY THE LIGHTING TO SIMULATE NIGHT OR DAY

You can change the mood simply by lowering the lights, shutting half of them off, using candlelight, or just toting along a lamp to cast the room into near darkness. However, be aware that you can also introduce naptime to your audience if you attempt this in the later afternoon, after a big meal, or in the evening. You don't want to hear someone snoring, so use with caution and only for short periods of time.

Many people lower the lights for their PowerPoint presentations, which can be a distraction especially for afternoon or evening presentations. Do you really need PowerPoint? Do you need all of the lights off in the room? Check beforehand how you can change the lighting in your venue to accommodate low-light requiring visual aids like PowerPoint.

Conversely, you can make your room brighter by opening blinds or curtains. If you notice that grey skies have cleared, you may want to share some sunshine with your audience on a previously gloomy day. It's a great pick-me-up for your audience's energy, and will likely foster added interaction too.

In appropriate situations, ask yourself: How can I change the atmosphere and the mood by changing the lights? It's fun and engages the audience on a different level when you adapt their atmosphere to your speech's objective.

Here are a couple examples…

1. Can you present by candlelight? It'd be a perfect choice if you were executing a Valentine's Day presentation about romantic dinner options and where to go.
2. If you're motivating the audience to get up earlier in the morning to grab a workout, then perhaps you'll want to make the room brighter.

Change the locale

Do you have to deliver a speech in a boardroom, classroom or training centre? Sometimes getting people outside of the usual venue for presentations can be stimulating!

Ask yourself: Can it be delivered more effectively elsewhere? Is there somewhere more appropriate for this message?

We've all seen this done in afternoon breakout sessions – let folks go outside and get some fresh air, or hold your presentation in the lunchroom as a lunch and learn.

Sometimes, shaking up the traditional choice of venue is what a speech needs to carry additional impact.

Another option is to shake up a room by moving people around. That way you can change how they look at things. You are the "Conductor," consider...

- How would it be best for you to deliver your speech?
- Do you need your audience to sit up on the tables so that they can look down on you in a classroom setting?
- Can you get some people to come up on stage to view the audience from that angle?

And when you just can't get away... asking your audience to close their eyes while you paint a word picture can be just as effective – it's just that simple. You could also use this creative step to set the stage for a shift in mood in the beginning or middle of your presentation. Just be careful that you don't ask the audience to close their eyes for too long as people get wary, bored, or may fall asleep.

I can remember presentations when the speaker spoke with such vivid and descriptive language that I could almost picture myself in their story -- sitting serenely at a café in Paris, or resting by a gushing waterfall. If you combine this step with the use of descriptive language, then the world is your oyster. You can take your audience virtually anywhere you want!

When you really want to draw in your audience, become a "word-artist" and craft for them a scene that they can see in their mind's eye. You can get started by crafting the desired word picture in your own mind by taking a moment to sit and recall, with all your senses, your personal experience. If you've ever taken an acting class you may have heard of Lee Strasberg's mood-setting technique used by actors called "Affective Memory." It's all about recalling places and experiences from the past, and you can learn more about it online.

How to Use Your Voice Creatively

Now, let's put on our Magic Speech Creator's Thinking Hat, and take a look at creativity from a public speaker's point of view.
If you struggle with being creative, then tap into the creativity of your circle of friends and ask them for ideas. There is nothing more boring than watching a speaker who didn't take the next step with their presentation by adding a little creative flair.

Can you remember watching someone present and thinking they need a poster, a PowerPoint presentation, or some music? As an audience member, I need to be SHOWN what they are talking about, by involving more than just my ears. There is a ton of information available online about different learning styles. I'm definitely a "show me don't just tell me" type of person and I know that many others are too.

It does not matter if you consider yourself to be creative or not, I assure you, we all possess innate creativity. I'm not talking about artistic ability. I'm not asking you to paint a backdrop or build a stage set, but to simply consider the #1 goal of any presentation - to be remembered.

In your speaker's toolbox, you have many choices of ways to enhance the creative presentation of any speech. Being a boring presenter is a poor choice. So, let's conduct a makeover on your creativity.

There are three ways to switch up your speech simply by the different use of your voice – we all have one, so it's the simplest way to make a big change in your speaking persona. You can change your...

- Words – use descriptive adjectives
- Language – don't use the same words over and over again
- Tone – the quality or character of your sound

🎁 GIFT TIP: Think for a minute on how you can vary these components in your everyday conversational speech to make your voice more creative, and watch for opportunities to incorporate those "Aha Moments" into your presentations.

Here are seven ways to spruce up your next presentation simply by using something I know you possess – your voice.

1. Stray from the median

Everybody has what is called a median voice range - it's your average voice or your conversational voice at your day-to-day speaking volume and pace. It's the way you would sound if you were to say "I'm going to get a cup of coffee."

In a presentation, you want to deviate from your median voice range in order to generate interest, as well as to emphasize key points. Going above the median by increasing your pace and volume will help you convey conviction and enthusiasm. Going below the median by decreasing your pace and volume will help you convey emphasis, drama, and a sense of thoughtfulness.

Nearly all speakers can improve their vocal quality. I recommend using a voice recorder regularly to record your presentations, or listening to recordings of others with your eyes closed to allow you to concentrate on the vocal quality. When reviewing how you sound, listen for ways to improve your vocal range, especially in the three key areas: words, language, and tone.

2. Word Emphasis

One of the best ways to change your inflection, the emphasis you place on individual words in a sentence, is to read a children's book. Have you ever read a Dr. Seuss book out loud? There is no way you can read it in one tone, at one speed, or at a median vocal level. So imagine your next speech was a Dr. Seuss book and pick out spots where you could vary your delivery. If you would like an example of this as inspiration, though no one expects you to emulate an actor, check out a YouTube video of Jim Carrey in How the Grinch Stole Christmas.

> 🎁 GIFT TIP: Reading to children is a great way to improve your vocal variety and presentation skills and can help you develop lively speech patterns and stretch your vocal skills. Try the Dr. Seuss book, Green Eggs and Ham and make it come alive for a child, or volunteer at your local library to read to the kids. Use changes in volume, pitch, and pace/speed to add excitement and enthusiasm to your stories.

Again, though we all detest the sound of our own voice, a recording can teach you much on your road of continuous improvement. I encourage you to have some fun with this exercise... and then translate some of that newfound vocal energy to your future presentations.

3. Try a whisper or a shout to shake up the audience's ears

You may have seen the movie, Ferris Bueller's Day Off and the scene where the history teacher asks a question followed by a droning "Anyone... anyone?" in a dead, flat monotone voice. If you recall the scene or can check it out on YouTube you will see that his boring voice has put his whole class to sleep. They've disengaged due to lack of a change in the teacher's inflection. In speaking, you definitely want to avoid a monotone vocal range at all costs as it will lull your audience to sleep.

Though a whisper works as well as a shout for gaining their attention, at the same time, you do not want to scare or startle your audience with an outburst or overly flamboyant presentation. I caution you to use this sparingly and only where it works appropriately. No one wants to be shouted at for a whole speech! But volume can also be used effectively to illustrate a point when it is utilized sparingly in a presentation.

Once you become adept at reading your audience's body language (more about how to do that coming up) you will know when you can insert an awakening and ear-opening vocal change to redirect their attention back to you.

I have experienced some speakers holding my attention in the palm of their hand and I absolutely adore this feeling of being spellbound by their voice and story. You may achieve this effect by reeling in your audience by lowering the pitch, volume, and speed of your delivery – not quite a whisper, but close.

Holding the audience in the palm of your hand is a big step towards your #1 goal in any speech – to be remembered. Ponder how you may be able to draw in your audience with quietly told stories that wrap themselves around your key message. I honestly believe when the audience reaches the point of being entranced by the presentation that this is the ultimate experience for both the presenter and the listener.

4. Choose a key word

Within your speech, you can use a specific word over and over again and make it the theme of your key message. One of my clients delivered a very creative speech all on the word "super," and how having a positive attitude propelled him forward in his successful career in sales. Every time I hear the word "super" I think of him. It was a speech about positivity in the workplace.

> **GIFT TIP:** Audiences love to learn new words from other languages. If you can weave such words into your presentation in a manner that is relevant, then use them to your advantage.

Another client delivered a speech about his favourite colour, yellow – also very memorable. The #1 goal is to be remembered. How can you build your whole speech around one keyword that will be planted into your listeners' minds? What word(s) would you choose?

5. Use onomatopoeia to your advantage

Onomatopoeia is a word that imitates or suggests the source of the sound that it describes. Certain words carry their characteristics i.e. SNAP, SMOOTH, SLOW. You cannot say snap slowly, nor can you say slowly fast -- it just doesn't sound right. Let your words take on their unique personalities. What other such words can you think of?

6. Try unique vocal variety

If you watch impersonators or actors like Jim Carrey (a favourite of mine, can you tell?), you will be inspired to utilize the full range of your voice. If you watch them the night before a presentation, they will definitely up your creativity the next day.

Famous actors such as Morgan Freeman and James Earl Jones are great examples of "vocal brands" because it's so very easy to distinguish their voices in any recording. What is your "brand?" Do you have something special about your voice? If you think not… ask a friend. They may surprise you. Our voices are as unique as our fingerprints!

Before delivering any speech, record yourself delivering your presentation. This is where owning a Smartphone comes in handy! To focus solely on your voice, close your eyes and listen first to WHAT you say (your words and language) for one playback. Then with your eyes still closed, run your playback a second time, and focus on HOW you say your speech (your tone and inflection).

- Where can you raise or lower your voice?
- Where can you stress a certain word more effectively?
- Where can you add a dash of creativity into your presentation with just your voice?

Finally, if you are truly unhappy with how you sound, it can be changed. However, your unique sound can be quite difficult to change unless you're willing to put in hours of quality practice time. This is especially important if you are looking to eliminate an accent or other speaking habits. With practice, perseverance and the assistance of a qualified speech therapist or a professional voice coach, a complete rebirth of your personal and unique sound is definitely possible.

You have all the tools you need to make big sweeping changes to how you stand out in a crowd of presenters, if you but harness the power of your own voice.

Four Criteria for Using Effective Visual Aids

It is very common - and somewhat expected - to support a presentation with visual aids. The most common crutch is PowerPoint. Once upon a time, although such aids were the height of creativity, they have slowly come to be expected and are therefore overused and often used very ineffectively, at least in my opinion.

There are many choices when it comes to visual aids, including: PowerPoint slides, overhead projectors, computer projection, flip charts, objects, video, role-plays, displays, and other media.

🎁 GIFT TIP: Incorporating video into a presentation is getting very popular and can be super simple and cost effective. However, it can also eat up time, especially if it is not cued up properly. Is there a video clip that totally enhances a presentation that you cannot live without? Keep video clips to less than 30 seconds if possible, or no more than 5% of your presentation. Attention wanes quickly when you have to turn down the lights.

It can be confusing and even intimidating for a speaker to consider all the alternatives for visual aids. Based on the hundreds of seminars I've experienced, and numerous interviews with presenters, I have identified four criteria that you need to consider for all visual aids, regardless of the medium.

1. Necessity

Give some thought to whether or not you actually need a visual aid. Since many people are visual learners, it is usually good to err on the side of using a visual aid rather that not using one.

Ask yourself: Will a visual aid enhance the audience's understanding of what I am saying? If the answer is yes, then use a visual aid. However, if you're using something like PowerPoint just because everyone else is… do without the hassle and headache of slides, break free of the stereotypical "crutch," and go without the gadgetry.

This strategy may sound harsh, but I have found most people use PowerPoint because they think they have to. Unfortunately, I have found that a large percentage misuse it and it ends up hurting their overall presentation.

The larger the audience, the bigger the visual has to be. I know that sometimes you can't help but use PowerPoint. But please… use it sparingly to showcase an image and don't fall into the trap of putting all your points on the screen and reading your speech from the computer monitor or screen. Remember that any well-used visual aid is an overview NOT a script, and is more intended for your listeners than for you. Also, ensure that your projected image fills the whole screen and does not hang off the sides.

2. *Clarity*

This criterion refers to clearness, or the best possible way to show what you have to say in a visual aid.

Ask yourself:

- What type of graphic would best express the data?
- What image or diagram would effectively show the subject matter, process or configuration?
- What keywords will best emphasize or highlight your message?

Visually displaying simple keywords may help your listeners remember a conclusion or essential steps in a process. Your challenge is to choose the best medium to support the idea you wish to express. For example…

- A simple column chart best expresses a change over time
- A pie chart best depicts a comparison of parts to a whole
- A historical timeline is helpful for linear thinkers
- A picture may be best when showing a building site or finished product

Be careful not to lose your audience in stats, instead a well-created chart outlining your main point can be effective. I especially love pie charts and bar graphs as they tell a quick "story." You can easily create some beautiful charts and graphs for your presentation using software like Microsoft Excel.

Consider using visual aids such as video recordings, role-plays, live demonstrations, or animation if these techniques best meet your needs. Consider whether you really need a visual aid, then think about clarity and the best way to support your words visually.

3. Simplicity

A picture may be worth a thousand words, but a picture of a thousand words isn't worth much, right? An effective visual should only express one core idea -- keep it simple. Don't confuse your audience by presenting a bunch of words, figures, and diagrams altogether on a visual. You can have too many pictures in your presentation so don't forget to edit down to the very best of the best -- less is more.

When using text visuals, such as a PowerPoint slide, use the rule of five. The number of lines per visual should be no more than five, and the number of words per line should not exceed five words. Some sources may recommend more than that, but I have found that seven to nine words per line or seven or nine lines per visual just clutters everything up and your audience ends up reading instead of listening. Remember, you don't want people to be reading a full statement; you just want to reinforce the spoken word. Show less, say more! My five-words/five-lines guideline forces you to focus and simplify, and that will make it easier for your viewers too.

Simplicity also applies to colour. Use colour to emphasize key points only. Too many colours complicate a visual. Again, you want your audience to focus on only one idea. Use colour to establish a focal point so the eyes of your listeners zero in on your key point. A visual aid that uses only one colour (or maybe two) for emphasis is very effective. More than that is distracting.

4. Readability

How many times have you been to a presentation where the speaker displayed a visual aid and said: "I know you can't read this, but let me tell you what it says?" Obviously, the speaker did not consider the criterion of visibility.

You can satisfy this criterion by choosing equipment and visuals that are:

- Appropriate to the room and audience size
- Proper placement of the equipment
- Design suitable media such as transparencies, slides, flip charts, or computer projection

In designing media to be projected, limit your choice of text styles to the family of sans serif fonts. Common sans serif fonts are Arial, Helvetica, and Geneva. These fonts are blocky and they project better than the serif family of fonts, like the Times New Roman font I'm using here. Choose point sizes that are 24 point or greater. The larger the better -- you want your audience to clearly see the text on the slides.

The best way to ensure visibility is to give your visual aids a test drive in the setting where you will be speaking. Evaluate visibility from all locations and angles in the room. It's important that everyone can see your visual aids; otherwise, they are worthless and can be a source of confusion and frustration.

Five More Creative Enhancements

Get Creative – Get Results – Get Remembered
Be Remembered – Be Asked to Speak Again

In addition to engaging the five senses, your voice, and visual aids, there are other tools to enhance your creativity and to stand out from the crowd. See if you can get your creative juices flowing for your next speech with the following examples. If you've used any other types of creative enhancements, I'd love to hear from you via social media. I'm always looking for more great examples to share with my clients and followers.

1. Costumes

Sometimes the best way to get your point across is by enhancing your personal presence with a costume. Doing so in a business setting can be tricky, though it could still be managed with any appropriate choice of apparel. Think of the late Steve Jobs' jeans and black turtleneck, which he used to emphasize a relaxed atmosphere for his presentations on Apple™ products. You'd never catch him presenting in a suit and tie!

As for professional male attire, if you need a suit and tie, then I recommend that you try to stand out in the crowd of blue and black outfits. Again the #1 goal is to be remembered. So guys, splurge on a brighter dress shirt or a tie that makes a statement. Ladies, make sure you're dressed for success with a great jacket or statement piece of large jewelry. This will also add to your confidence – look great, feel great, present great!

What do you have around the house, or that you could easily borrow or buy to enhance the topic of your speech? Going back to our salsa example, do you think that wearing a sombrero would enhance or distract from a speech about salsa?

For another example, I remember traveling on an airplane many years ago when the flight attendants donned Groucho Marx glasses complete with noses and mustaches to get the attention of passengers during the usually dull pre-flight safety announcements. How creative is that? I loved it!

2. Pictures

Is there one image that sums up what you are discussing? Perhaps that is the image you should use to open or close your presentation. Sometimes leaving the audience with a powerful image at the end of your speech can cement your message. Google™ images and social media websites like Pinterest™ provide amazing ways to incorporate images into a presentation.

If someone has never been to a tropical rainforest and therefore has not seen the lushness of the vegetation you are discussing in your travel presentation, then projecting a picture on a screen can be very powerful. If you are going to discuss your idol or mentor, I suggest having a photo of them to show your listeners as it brings that person to life for them.

3. Handouts

Again, handouts are a double-edged sword and can contribute to audience distraction if not used properly. With paper conservation in mind, I advocate a handout be no more than one sheet of paper, double-sided if you must. Go for a coloured piece of paper as opposed to white. If you must use white paper, print in coloured ink if you can. At the very least, highlight a few key points in bold or with a highlighter pen.

🎁 GIFT TIP: With websites and unique webpages so easy to create, perhaps all you need to provide your listeners is an odd-shaped or colourful business card that will stand out in a pile of other handouts with the appropriate URL listed for them to reference at their convenience.

4. Reward Them

If you find the attention of the audience waning or you want to encourage participation, a little food bribe or present works every time, especially if you can make the giveaway relevant to your presentation.

I attended a Disney Institute seminar where the speaker gave away a small Disney figurine to anyone who asked a good question. I firmly believe in the theory that you get more of what you reward! And, they did get a ton of interactivity and questions in that session. Everyone wanted a memento to commemorate his or her attendance.

For example, if you want participation when you ask a question... simply reward it with a piece of Halloween candy. If you need to encourage asking question at the end of your presentation...

provide a desirable token for anyone who asks a question. That's because people perk up and get competitive when they know that there is something in it for their participation.

Ask yourself: *What could I use to tie into my presentation?*

Going back to my Salsa Recipe example, I could easily fling out packets of pre-measured spices for a "just add tomatoes" prize to reward participation. Or I could pop around with a personal-sized sample plate to reward engaged listeners with a taste-test of the salsa before everyone else.

5. Be Mysterious with Your Ending

Sometimes keeping the audience guessing, when done well, creates a very intriguing "who done it" atmosphere that engages the listeners to play along to see if they can figure out where the speech is taking them. You wouldn't want to use this technique in longer speeches, but people will sit on the edge of their seats to find out a happy or interesting ending when you build the suspense effectively.

As you can see, creativity can take many forms. You have probably been inspired to come up with some new ones too. Let the sky be the limit when it comes to thinking outside of that tired old box. There is a ton of information available online so play around on Google or whatever search engine you use and see what you can come up with when you type in Creative Speech Writing.

11

Debunking the Practice Makes Perfect Myth

A great goal is to practice at least three times a day for a week prior to your actual presentation. Practice should not take the form of standing in the boardroom or on stage and repeating your same words over and over again to get them "just right." In this chapter, I will share some practice strategies that can be utilized almost anywhere and in a variety of ways in your busy schedule.

Before we move on, I'd like to extract a promise from you... I'll share more tips throughout this chapter, but note that practicing does not mean reading your speech, aloud and verbatim, from ten pages of typewritten notes. As you have read, I teach my clients to be spontaneous and let their thoughts flow naturally from a sketched outline. Using your one-page outline and no other notes, prepare your presentation by actually doing your presentation. Use your practice time wisely to talk, not write, your speech. I'm asking you trust me on this because I've seen it work hundreds, if not thousands of times already!

In addition to verbal practice, regular visualization of your success is important too! Picture yourself (at least once a day) having a conversation with the audience. If you're not a believer in the power of visualization, you will be by the end of this chapter!

Finally, this chapter will explore the concept of a dress rehearsal. Plan your practice time to give yourself a trial run at home and see how you do. This is an actual test-run with family and friends. After a powerful dress rehearsal, you can tweak your presentation just like the actors in a play do in their dry run. It's especially powerful if your listeners can record you on their smartphones from a variety of angles so that you get a well-rounded perspective of how you move throughout your space.

When I recently complimented a speaker on their smooth performance, they replied, "It was easy, because I had done it a hundred times, though never in front of an audience." Simply visualizing your presentation regularly can be helpful. Seeing yourself, in your mind's eye, smoothly presenting a great speech can make the same thing come true in real life.

Try to work a few mental run-throughs into your practice time, and picture yourself giving an amazing presentation -- and you will do just that!

> 🎁 GIFT TIP: If you can't hold a live dress rehearsal in the actual space, then use added visualization exercises.

Overcoming Fear Using Visualization
- My Story -

When I was a young girl, I was a competitive figure skater. To be good at figure skating, you have to have zero fear of falling. Unfortunately, falling and breaking bones was my #1 fear. To progress through the various levels in figure skating, you have to be able to complete jumps of multiple revolutions up in the air and land on one foot on a skinny little blade. I knew immediately that this meant that I was going to fall -- a lot -- while learning complicated jumps.

This is a great analogy to learning any type of slightly dangerous new activity or skill. If you've ever watched a figure skating competition on television, you know that most high-level competitors are doing triple and quadruple rotating jumps in their programs. But we all start off with our first nemesis – the Axel jump - one and a half rotations in the air.

The axel is the only jump that you take off from a forward outside edge and land on a backward outside edge. It's very scary to literally throw yourself up into the air with the hope of landing safely 100% of the time. (Hmmm... just like public speaking!) Plus, I'm sure you can picture how thin a skate blade is... about 1/8th of an inch. I was determined to conquer that jump so that I could move on to the next level and learn something new!

I had been working on the jump for months and months and I was so frustrated that I couldn't figure out how to land my nemesis, the axel. My coach offered me $20 to land the jump. But...I had to land the jump by the next day or the deal was off. At 9 years of age, $20 was a lot of money -- so I was motivated! Not only did I want to move on, but now I had an added incentive to succeed.

The night before, I remember sitting comfortably in my bedroom with my eyes closed and in my mind's eye I "saw" myself landing the jump. Moreover, I "felt" myself landing the jump. I replayed that scene over and over again in my head. I saw myself skating backwards, readying myself to jump, stepping onto my jumping edge, taking off, spinning quickly in the air, tucking my arms in appropriately, unwrapping my leg, and landing the jump perfectly. I saw the whole thing in my head, and for some strange reason,

> maybe I was just naïve, I believed that the next day when I stepped onto the ice rink that I would land my axel on the first try.
>
> Do you know what happened the next day? I did it! I conquered my nemesis, amazed my coach (and myself) and made $20 – mission accomplished. That is the power of visualization.

What would motivate you to present successfully?

_____

_____

_____

_____

Are you an adrenaline junkie that simply loves to conquer the fear of anything you've not yet tried? Sometimes, when it's fear that stands between you and accomplishing a goal, you just have to put on your Nike hat and adopt their philosophy, "Just Do It."

I encourage you to give visualization a try to enhance your public speaking confidence. The more confidence you feel you need, the more you should be utilizing daily visualization exercises.

Visualize Yourself Presenting

Here's an exercise that you can try the next time to prepare for a presentation.

Find yourself a quiet place where you can be still for a few minutes. If this is before a class or work presentation, try sitting in your car, using a quiet bathroom stall, or find a private room.

Close your eyes and relax your body and mind. Take deep breaths and focus on a pinpoint of light in your mind's eye.
It's helpful to visit your presentation space before you speak so that you can visualize more accurately.

Now, see yourself approaching the stage/lectern/podium/microphone.

See yourself facing your audience and watch yourself take one last deep breath before you begin to speak.

Experience a surge of confidence as you open your mouth to speak your first word.

Watch yourself begin your speech; hear the strength in your voice; view the audience's positive reaction to your words.

Continue picturing your presentation throughout the body of your message. Feel your speech flow from your memory. View the reactions of the audience to your highlights and key points. Envision them sitting raptly and taking notes. Experience your entire presentation as if you were in front of them right now.

As you witness yourself drawing your presentation to a close, visualize the type of ending you desire. How do you want your presentation to end? I want you to visualize that right now.

- Would you like a flurry of hands eagerly rising to ask questions or to sign up for your offer?
- Do you want everyone to pause a moment after your last word and then break into applause?
- Can you see them giving you a standing ovation?

Repeat this visualization exercise several times. Each time try to incorporate all of your senses.

- How bright is the room?
- What does it smell like?
- How is the audience dressed?
- Are you feeling warm or chilly?
- Is there drinking water present?
- How does it taste as you take a sip prior to opening your presentation?
- Is the room so quiet that you can hear the ventilation system?
- How solid is the lectern or table that you are using to hold your notes? Does it rock or move or shake when you put weight on it?

Manifesting Success

Another kind of visualization is known as manifesting. I learned about this through the 2006 movie The Secret, which is based on the book of the same name. Once you set an intention or goal, you simply have to live and talk like it is happening in the present and forget all the negativity of the past. I'm not going to get into all the nitty-gritty details about how it all works; you can watch the movie or read the book to learn more about the law of attraction. But simply stated… setting the wheels in motion towards accomplishing any goal or dream starts with believing in yourself. You can achieve what you set out to do, but the first step is to simply believe strongly that you can do it.

Seven Steps to "Perfect" Practice

Follow these seven steps between now and the time you present… because practice doesn't make perfect, but near perfect practice will definitely boost your self-confidence once you step on the stage.

1. Jump right in

Using your outline, give your presentation at home. Don't worry about writing your speech out in full - trust me - just present it from your outline. You can present to a pet, or a child's stuffed animal, but please no real people at this stage. Time yourself just to see how long it takes, but do not video or audio record your presentation – yet.

2. Tweak it

Next, ask yourself, "How did your first run go?" Then take the time to tweak your presentation on paper.

Ask yourself… What went well? What didn't go so well? What should I do differently? Makes some notes here or in your speaking journal.

_____

_____

_____

_____

_____

SECOND RUN

Present your speech again. Does it feel better the second time around? Does it need more tweaking? Perhaps the third time's the charm? If so, give it a third run, or as many as you need to smooth out your outline.

4. Time to record

Now that you've got two or three run-throughs under your belt, it's time to record yourself in action. Ask a friend to video you, or set up your iPhone or other device. Audio recording is fine for this step as well. Use my "Self-Evaluation Questionnaire" in Chapter 13 to review your recording and analyze areas where you could be stronger.

5. Tweak & repeat

By now, you should pretty much know what you want to say and how you want to say it. Now, it's time to polish your presentation! If you drive to work alone, you may want to recite it in the car. Where else could you be practicing your presentation without notes?

_____

_____

_____

_____

🎁 GIFT TIP: I suggest a perfect place to run through your speech is in the shower – no soggy notes allowed. Works like a charm. For many, the shower is the only time and place that you may stand still and be alone throughout a busy day.

6. Dress rehearsal

Like any great production, the night before you present, you will want to do a dry run. Practice your complete presentation from the set up through to the end without stopping. You may want to get into costume as well. The key at this stage of your practice process is to go through your whole presentation from start to end without stopping to make adjustments or notes for changes.

If your speech is still not running smoothly, then you may require more practice. If you haven't conducted a video review then try to do so as it too can be helpful. And, depending on the importance, you may wish to conduct more than one dress rehearsal just to smooth out the last of the bugs.

7. The big day

It's the big day, and you're all set. You're confident! You're prepared! You're polished! You've visualized success, and now presenting is the least of your worries -- because you're ready!

PRACTICE TIME SUGGESTIONS

How much time someone should practice a presentation depends on the individual and the importance of the event. Three times a day for shorter presentations is quite do-able, as long as, in the end, the presentation doesn't come off too polished. If so it can appear robotic, slick, or lacking in authenticity.

Levels of practice include:

- Sub-vocal i.e. in your head
- Vocal i.e. spoken aloud by yourself
- Vocal before a video camera
- Vocal before an informal audience
- Vocal before a test run audience and video recorded
- Full dress rehearsal on location

You may find that many business presentations are requested on very short notice. As a professional speaker, I usually find myself with weeks or months to prepare to speak, but I know that is not the case for most speakers. Most speakers usually have limited time and therefore must rely only on a quick sub-vocal practice.

You will find a practice session of any kind very valuable to your performance. Practice until you feel comfortable with the content of your speech and with any equipment you will be using. However, don't practice so much that you begin to get bored with your own presentation. You want to keep your enthusiasm for the subject matter high, as that enthusiasm will be contagious with your listeners!

As already stated, it's valuable to practice your presentation in the room where you will be speaking if you can. This allows you to get a feel for the room and can greatly add to your confidence. Test the many variables you have included in your speech (e.g. pauses, eye contact and range, visual aids, etc.) Not only will you have the opportunity to practice using your props or visual aids to ensure they project properly, but you can also practice using any sound equipment in the room that will be used during the presentation. You can also rehearse any stage movements you are planning. An added benefit to this type of practice is that it creates a mental image you can use over and over again to visualize your success, no matter where or how you are practicing.

🎁 GIFT TIP: If you can, go visit the actual room/stage as early as you can – days, weeks, months before because there may be things within your presentation that you would change right from the start of the planning process. You should be aiming to present the most effective way possible based on the room constraints. After all, no one likes last minute surprises!

Video Recording Review Guidelines

If I haven't hit you over the head enough regarding the importance of continuous improvement in your public speaking persona, then let me stress one more time that you should record all of your dress rehearsals and absolutely all of your live presentations. There is little need to hire a speech coach if you learn how to effectively evaluate each and every one of your own presentations.

Growth is not a quick process, so you will need to run through your video at least four times, five if you really wish to improve your personal speaking style fast.

🎁 GIFT TIP: Never watch the video right after your presentation or if you're tired. It will skew your perception.

Video is a great tool, just like reading this book and using feedback and assistance from a speech coach. However, it's harder to take in constructive feedback when your energy is low. Organize your review and evaluation time carefully as part of your overall speech-crafting plan. Remember to take it easy on yourself and not be super critical of your presentation.

Normal

Watch your video at normal speed and volume -- just to satisfy your curiosity. Remember, almost no one (including me) likes to see themselves on video, but this is an excellent way to jump-start your public speaking upgrading! So just grin and bear it.

Ears Open - Eyes Shut

This next run through can be one of the most powerful lessons to learn how to quickly improve your presentation. Watch the video with your eyes closed and concentrate on how you sound.

- Count your thinking noises (um's and uh's, etc.)
- How was your tone, pace, volume, vocal variety, relaxation in your voice, breathing?
- Can you hear any other noises from the lectern, your feet, or hands?
- What words or phrases did you continually repeat throughout your speech?
- How can you change your words, language, and tone?

Fast Forward

In the good ol' days of the VCR machine this was an incredible tool!

Today, it's a bit trickier to record as effectively on a smartphone. You may need to transfer the file to a film-creation App or to your computer to utilize this feature. The bigger the screen you can view it on, the better.

First, you should be able to see yourself clearly while the video fast forwards. Watching yourself slightly sped up allows you to view any erratic, repetitive gestures or movements.

Ask yourself these questions…

- Did you pace like a caged tiger?
- Were you dancing in one place, or moving with purpose?
- What else do you notice about your speedier self?

Sound-Off

Turn the sound off completely so that you can focus on watching just your body language while you watch your video. Remember 55% of what you communicate is non-verbal. Keep Chapter 9 of this book open to review the five key body language areas – stance, movement, gestures, eye contact, and facial expressions.

What do you notice?

_____

_____

_____

_____

Normal Again

I know that this procedure seems long…but watch your video one more time in order to put it all back together in your head. Answer these debriefing questions after every presentation, both before you review the video as well as afterwards...

- What went well?
- What went wrong?
- What would you do differently next time?

Take notes in your speaking journal on where you want to make personal improvements for your next presentation. Remember as Walt Disney said... *"If you are not growing, you're dying. If you're coasting... you're going downhill!"* Don't be a "coaster." Continuous improvement is the secret to amazing public speaking success! A speaking journal is a great place to keep all that learning together in one easy to reference book.

12

Ummmm, Eliminating Thinking Noises

My biggest pet peeve when it comes to watching speeches/presentations is the big, bad thinking noise, also known as the "Ummmm."

These are the annoying and distracting sounds that everyone makes when their mouth gets one step ahead of their brain. When did it become not only okay but socially acceptable to stammer through a speech littered with thinking noises? Somewhere along the line society has said that it is okay to sound unintelligent, unprepared, and unconfident. That is what people really think when they hear these silence-filling word crutches and they tune out whatever you are saying when you repetitively utilize them.

After hearing thousands of client speeches, I wrote this chapter to help you reduce the use of these filler words in your vocabulary, and in the speech of tomorrow's leaders, our children. To be taken seriously in the business world, one must learn to talk like a corporate CEO – grab some YouTube videos of those Fortune 500 A-listers. Once you gain the respect of your listeners you will open yourself to many new and wondrous opportunities. So let's retire the "ummmm" together, shall we?

Defining Your Personal Thinking Noise

A thinking noise is ANY word that is repeated (without meaning) more than a few times in a conversation or presentation. When the audience hears your repetitive thinking noise over and over again, they become distracted and may begin to count how many you use.

The most common of these words are the "um's" and "uh's," but they can also include:

☐ and	☐ like	☐ that
☐ anyways	☐ okay	☐ and then
☐ basically	☐ really	☐ well
☐ hmmm	☐ right	☐ you know
☐ huh	☐ so	… and many others

Before you can eliminate these pesky thinking noises, you need to know what your personal thinking noises are. Listen to yourself as you speak in everyday conversations listen for the repetitive words you use when you pause to think out loud. Record yourself or ask someone you trust to listen carefully in order to help you identify your thinking noise(s).

We all use one or more of these thinking noise words in our everyday conversations. Do you already know what your thinking noise is? If so, write it below.

_____

Release the Butterflies and Become Fearless

One cause of the thinking noises is stage fright. Presenters, for some reason, think that the audience is there to see them fail. Contrary to popular belief, most audience participants want to see their time well spent watching a successful presenter. When you watch your favourite sports team or music concert... do you want to see them fail? No. So, why should your "performance" be any different in the eyes of your listeners?

Your initial and final impressions are the most important, so I'm a big advocate of practicing your introduction and your conclusion more than the other 80% of your speech -- the body. As long as you reiterate your points three times, the key message you wish to communicate will be cemented in your listeners' minds. But if they tune-out during your introduction period where you're rambling, stuttering, and using copious thinking noises, they may not listen to anything else you have to say.

Practice your introductory remarks so that you perfect a fluid opening that will give your butterflies time to settle down and set you on a course for success. If your whole speech is less than 15 minutes in length, then you can easily conduct a practice run through at least three times a day. Can you INVEST 45 minutes a day in yourself for a week or two?

Be Prepared for the Unexpected

There is no bigger "virus of the thinking noises" than having to give an impromptu speech, or when you haven't taken the time to fully prepare a presentation.

The easiest solution is to always be prepared, especially in business situations. If you always expect that you will be asked to speak, then you will always have something smooth to say. Take a couple of minutes to collect your thoughts before...

- Walking into a meeting
- Addressing the media
- Business networking
- Speaking at a social event, such as a wedding

A great habit to develop is thinking of your main point, as well as two to three sub-points to support your stance or argument, especially for impromptu presentations. You can practice this in your everyday conversations.

Don't Try to Eat the Whole Elephant

As you saw at the beginning of this book, one of my favourite trick questions is "How do you eat an elephant? Why... one bite at a time of course!" Otherwise, it is too overwhelming – just like public speaking. This helpful bit of advice also applies to changing any habit including eliminating your big, bad thinking noise.
Start by trying to avoid using thinking noises at least 10% of the time. Work your way up to eliminating them at least half the time during regular in-person conversations, or just for a whole morning. You will notice that they may leave you forever as soon as you begin to concentrate on avoiding those filler words.

Soon, you will find yourself making presentations without using any thinking noises at all, even when presenting long speeches or training sessions.

It's a Habit That Can be Broken

You need to consciously correct your language choices. As with changing any habit, you need to persevere and be tough on yourself for at least 28 days. That's 24 hours a day and 7 days a week, not just when you are presenting a speech!

Here are six strategies you can start using right now to consciously correct your language choices...

1. Bite your tongue or take a deep breath instead of saying "ummmm," especially when you lose your train of thought
2. Clench your teeth instead of saying "like"
3. Practice your presentation and ask a friend to count your thinking noises for you
4. Play a game with your family, friends, or co-workers by

putting a dollar in a "Thinking Noise Jar" every time you are caught filling the air with any thinking noise
5. Have someone mimic your thinking noise every time you use it
6. Snap an elastic band around your wrist every time you use a thinking noise in regular conversations

Treat Presentations as Conversation

Avoid using thinking noises in everyday conversations. Then when presenting, you can concentrate on just having another 'conversation' with the audience. It's a small mindshift that pays big dividends but it takes self-discipline.

You can do this by asking your audience questions to stimulate two-way communication. If you're feeling nervous at the outset, opening your presentation with a few questions can also settle you into the presentation right away. If you can converse easily one-on-one with a stranger or an acquaintance, then, with only a little bit more practice, you should be able to become an effective public speaker to a larger group by using those same principles.

Handkerchief Method

Buy a large box of J-Cloth's (blue kitchen dish cloths) or colourful Kleenex and hand them to someone in the front row. Every time you "ummmm" or use any thinking noise, ask your volunteer to throw one of them up into the air for you and everyone else to see. For a low-key approach, you can ask them to drop the clothes/tissues on the carpet after a slight wave to get your attention each time you use your thinking noise. It's very effective! One client used it and cut down her thinking noises from 40+ to less than 5 just by using this helpful reminder.

Recently, one of my clients handed me a box of light plastic Ping-Pong balls before her test presentation to a small group. She asked me to throw one ball at her for each of her "um's." Such a fun and creative idea, right? She went from 20+ "um's" for her first speech to only 2 in her second presentation.

Breathe and Make Eye Contact

Let Silence Be Golden! One of the biggest reasons for thinking noises is that we have become uncomfortable with silence.

When you practice your presentation, if you remember to pause for a breath, you will not only control your pace and slow down (and avoid turning blue) -- you will also avoid utilizing thinking noises. I have yet to meet anyone who can talk and breathe at the exact same time. This suggestion works well in conjunction with biting your tongue when you're in the learning stages.

Props Give You Confidence

I actually get worried when my clients are NOT nervous, because overconfidence can potentially be as fatal as nervousness. Most speakers are nervous and that is simply biological and natural.

Visual aids can work like a charm to calm your nerves! During the first 1 to 2 minutes of a speech, most presenters just want to clutch their notes, or the lectern -- it's a typical reaction to the stress of facing down a room full of eyeballs. By planning to hold an opening prop, the speaker can clutch a prop instead, and begin their presentation with a show and tell. Begin your speech design by thinking of which type of prop you could use in your introduction so that your hands have something to do, and the audience's eyes have something to focus upon other than just you.

In my 6-week or 4-day courses, the first presentation my clients prepare is their demonstration (or informative) speech. This type of speech provides the speaker something to do with their hands – hold a prop. Just about anything you can hold in your hands - including any items that have a special significance to the topic of the presentation can help maintain your focus and give you something to do (i.e. look at) instead of using a thinking noise. When used strategically, a relevant prop can also provide added strength to you and your presentation, especially if it is a special or significant life marker like a trophy or other memento of a major moment in your life.

Props can take many forms including:

- Mementos of your travels like postcards and souvenirs
- Inspirational items
- Photographs
- Knick-knacks and collectibles, etc.

🎁 GIFT TIP: If your prop is a picture and you are using flimsy paper... glue it to a stiff piece of cardboard which will hide any nervous shakes!

Use Voicemail to Your Advantage

Voice mail is the perfect place to begin practicing how to eliminate your thinking noises each and every day! Most people now use voice mail in one form or another, whether on your cell phone, at home, or in the office – it's everywhere! We all despise rambling voice mail messages that waste our precious time. Mastering voice mail messaging is a great first step to learning to communicate concisely. Know what you are going to say even before you dial the phone number. Think of the main or most important point of your message before you dial someone so that you can state this message if you get their voice mail.

Similar to email, there is usually a way to record a message and review it before you send it. Check for instructions with your specific system and then practice reviewing your recordings prior to walking away from the phone. Listen especially for your thinking noises or word whiskers.

- Do you repeat "and then" over and over? Or any other word repeatedly after the word "and."

- Are you using the word "like" just to fill thinking time that should remain silent?
- Are you "ummmm'ing" and "uhhhh'ing" repeatedly?

If so, then re-record the message without the thinking noises before you send it to the recipient.

🎁 GIFT TIP: For outgoing voice mail message, use a script and record your message standing up!

Be Present

When you feel that you are getting ahead of your thoughts, take a deep, cleansing breath, make solid, confident eye contact with the audience, and then continue when you are ready. Force yourself to be present!

If you're feeling lost in your presentation, either recap the points you just covered, or move onto your next topic instead of using one of those pesky thinking noises.

When you are making eye contact, conduct a quick body language survey of the audience – is there something they are trying to tell you?

Preparation and Practice

When thinking noises, like your own personal presentation plague, haunt you then you need to take absolutely every minute or hour you have to prepare. Use any preparation time you are allotted wisely to plan a successful presentation. Use any extra practice time, wherever you can grab it because "real practice" will eliminate any thinking noises in your speech.

Know that your listeners are on your side… until you let your credibility slip by using thinking noises. Even the best presenters sometimes stumble through their opening remarks, so try to start strong and go forward the same way throughout your presentation.

I'm a procrastinator, but I find this quotation "Procrastination is the fear of success" by Dennis Waitley works as a kick in the butt to get me started. He goes on to say,

"People procrastinate because they are afraid of the success that they know will result if they move ahead now. Because success is heavy, carries a responsibility with it, it is much easier to procrastinate and live on the 'someday I'll' philosophy."

Though you may already be sick and tired of hearing me talk about it… the easiest way to get rid of thinking noises is to practice, practice, practice – and practice not using them.

By eliminating thinking noises, you will sound more intelligent, be more prepared, and most importantly you will be able to effectively communicate your message in a clear and non-distracting manner.

Please promise me that, no matter where you are or what you are doing, that you will practice eliminating those nasty thinking noises. Perhaps, my pet peeve has now become one of your top pet peeves and that will help you to pay it forward to other people you know. One day we WILL banish the "ummmm!"

Do you have a creative suggestion to beat this habit? Please feel free to post them on my Facebook Page at www.Facebook.com/GoodToGreatPS

13

Speech Evaluation Strategies

This is where we take all the hints, tips, and strategies of public speaking and put them all together. This chapter contains the width and breadth of speaking elements that a formal speech evaluator will be looking for. I've developed these evaluation criteria over the past decade in order to objectively and fairly grade each of my clients on their presentations.

When I first studied public speaking as part of my marketing communications program, my near-retirement instructor, in my opinion, was a bit lazy when it came to grading. She simply gave us a mark out of 10 with very little feedback or breakdown about where improvements could be made. When I graduated and was asked to return to my college to teach public speaking, the first thing I did was create a fair and detailed evaluation scale that would grade the students in many different areas for each speech presentation.

Evaluation Criteria for Speakers

Using the following scale, rank each of the criteria below

    0 = Not completed or attempted
    1 = Weakly completed (provide your suggestions for improvements)
    2 = Partially completed (provide your suggestions for improvements)
    3 = Completed but lacking slightly (provide your suggestions for improvements)
    4 = Good, could use a small final polish (provide your suggestions for improvements)
    5 = Excellent, video review suggested to fine-tune minor improvements

You are building your foundation as a speaker. Your goal is to not receive perfect fives on each of these evaluation points, but to benchmark your first few presentations. The list sounds like a lot to think about during a short time period while you're presenting, but pick two or three to focus on with each practice run through and you'll soon find yourself "ace-ing" a formal evaluation.

Remember, you only have to change the things you wish to change – you don't have to incorporate every criterion, only the ones that you think will apply to your presentation. Once again, How do you Eat an Elephant? -- try changing just one thing at a time until it becomes natural, and don't try to eat that whole elephant in just one bite. True speaking persona evolution takes time!

___ Answering Questions
- What was your level of comfort in answering the audience's questions?

___ Audience Involvement
- Did you grab their attention?
- Did listeners appear interested in your presentation?
- Were their eyes focused on you during your speech?

___ Audience Receptivity
- Did they look like they wanted to ask questions throughout your presentation?
- Were they leaning forward in their seats?

___ Balance of Points
- Were your points well balanced time-wise?
- Did your chosen order seem logical?

___ Body Language and Stance
- Were you standing comfortably?
- Were you well balanced?
- Were your feet shoulder-width apart?
- What were your hands doing when you didn't need them to show something or gesture?
- Were your arms down at your sides?
- Did you smile?
- Did you engage with some of the audience using eye contact?
- Did your body language communicate confidence and enhance your audience's belief in your knowledge of the topic?

___ Breathing and Voice
- Did your voice carry throughout the room?
- Were you speaking from your diaphragm and projecting your words?
- Did you ever seem out of breath?

___ Conclusion
- Did you allow sufficient time to wrap up your speech?
- Did you give us an action step or tell us how we could get started doing this ourselves?
- Did you reiterate your three main points?

___ Conversation Starter
- Did you use a conversation starter to pull us into your speech?

- Did you give us an opportunity to react to your topic before moving on to the body of your presentation?
- Did you arouse the listener's interest from the start of your speech?

___ Conversing
- Did you involve your audience in the conversation throughout your presentation?
- Was conversation well incorporated into this speech?

___ Creative Word Choices
- Did you use carefully chosen words to explain concepts?

___ Creativity
- Were there unique aspects to the delivery of your speech?

___ Credibility
- Was your level of emotional commitment and personal knowledge/experience effectively communicated?
- Did you share your experience level with the audience?

___ Eye Contact
- How often were you reading from your notes?
- Did you break eye contact with your audience members too often by looking at walls, floor, ceiling?
- Did you spread your eye contact around the room or did you focus on one person?

___ Follow-up Material
- Did your follow up material reinforce important facts and provide the audience with the next actionable step?
- Was it concise and eye catching?

___ Gesturing
- Were effective gestures used throughout the entirety of the speech?

- Were your gestures distracting?
- Did you gesture too much? Or too little?

___ Introduction/Three Points

- Did you include your three main points in your introductory remarks?
- Was your introduction only 10% of your speech length?
- Was the key message clearly stated in your introduction?

___ Limited Use of Notes

- Did you place your notes on the tabletop or lectern?
- Did you hold them in your hands?
- Were notes used sparingly?

___ Logical Order

- Was your speech clearly and logically organized?
- Did your speech progress from providing basic information to educating your listeners on your viewpoint?

___ Memorable Presentation

- When we hear your topic mentioned will we think of you?
- Can we easily recall your three main points in the future?
- Did you provide a handout to jog the audience's memory later?

___ Movement

- How was your movement?
- Did you get physically closer to your audience?
- Did you stand still throughout your speech?
- Did you build in an opportunity to move?
- Did you set up a portion of your presentation a few steps away from your "safety zone?"

___ Pace and Speed of Delivery
- Were you hard to understand because you spoke too fast at times?
- Did you take time to breathe?
- Was there a pause between ideas to allow the audience to digest what you were saying?

___ Persuasiveness
- Was the speech persuasive?
- Was the audience convinced?
- Was there a thought provoking zinger?

___ Preparation
- Did you look like you spent time on your presentation?
- Did it look like you just put it together last night?
- Did you finish on time?

___ Props and Visual aids
- Did you use props effectively?
- Did they meet all four criteria - Necessity, Clarity, Simplicity, and Visibility?
- Were your props large enough for all the audience members to see?
- Were your visual aids legible and easy to read?
- Did visual aids add to the presentation, or did you find them inappropriate or overly abundant?

___ References
- Were you able to make a reference to topical information or a previous speaker's speech?

___ Relaxation and Comfort
- Did you seem comfortable with your topic and what you were demonstrating?
- Did your expertise shine through?

___ Speech Title

- Did the choice of title for this presentation seem to come from "outside the box?"
  - Did the title catch our attention?
  - Could it have been improved upon?

___ Support

- Were each of your three main points supported with sufficient evidence?
- Did you insert bits of personal experience using your own stories to make the topic come alive?
- Did you make an emotional appeal?

___ Timing

- Where did the speech wrap up, was it as close to the maximum time as possible?
- How much time was left on the clock?
- Did you go overtime?

___ Thinking Noises and Flow

- Was your presentation smooth?
- Did you use um/uh/ands throughout your presentation, or were you present in the moment?
- Did you carry your enthusiasm for the topic throughout your presentation?

___ Tone and Vocal Variety

- Did you speak with inflection?
- Did you stress important points by raising your voice slightly?
- Did you possess a sing-songy cadence in your speaking rhythm?
- Was there were sufficient change in your pitch and tone of voice throughout your speech?

___ What's In It for Me?
- Did you communicate to your audience the main reason why they should pay attention to your speech?
- Should the audience care about your topic?

___ Zinger Finale
- Was your zinger memorable?
- How creative was the final statement, and did it lend itself well to finishing off your presentation strongly?

Constructive Speech Critiquing Others

The following is an exercise to increase your learning. I encourage you to use these questions to immediately review a presentation. If you cannot find one to experience in-person, then check out YouTube to find a speech to watch. Try to avoid the high-profile speaking professionals for this mini assignment.

Consider these points and then spend some time writing a critique of the speaker's presentation in your speaking journal.

- Did you like the speaker's title for the presentation? What would you have named it?
- What went well for the speaker? What two things did you like the most about their presentation?
- What seemed to be the speaker's biggest strength? Was there only one? Explain.
- Did the speaker appear to be having fun? Why or why not? Give at least two examples of how they demonstrated they were enjoying their topic.
- How was the speaker's movement? Did they walk toward or into the audience or did they stay behind the lectern/counter/table? What would you suggest that they do differently in this regard? Draw a movement map from the start to the end of the speech showing their pattern of movement throughout their speech.

- One a scale of 1 (low) to 10 (high), how engaged were you and the audience in this topic/speaker? What thing(s) seemed to move, touch, or grab the audience's attention the most?
- If the speech was shorter than the allotted time, what do you think the speaker could have added to enhance their presentation and fill the remaining time?
- How did the speaker demonstrate creativity? (i.e. visual aids, word choices, vocal variety, etc.)
- How were the speaker's "thinking noises?" Did you notice them? Were there many? How would you suggest that they rectify this problem?
- Did the speaker distract you with anything that they did or said? What was your overall impression of their body language?

Self-Evaluation Questionnaire

Now it's your turn! Hopefully, you have a speech to deliver soon. In the 24 to 48 hours after you present, sit down and answer the following questions for yourself. Remember to save self-critical evaluation like this for when you're ready (not tired).

Record your answers to each of these questions in your speaking journal. This is a great way to keep all your impressions of speeches, both of yourself and of others together in one place. A speaking journal is also an awesome tool for jotting down topic ideas and/or revelations.

> 🎁 GIFT TIP: Trust me...one day, you will want to look back on your humble beginnings along the path of becoming a successful presenter and remember the good ol' days!

1. Did I cover all the points I planned to cover? If I left out a point, was it crucial to the talk? Or am I being a perfectionist?

2. Did I get an initial response right away? What was it? Was it the response I wanted? Did it bring the audience closer to me?
3. Did I get additional responses I hadn't counted on? Did I allow responses to become too lengthy, or did I cut them off by rushing to my next point?
4. Was it fun? Why? Why not?
5. Did I stay with my outline? If I went off of it, when did it happen? Did something good come of that?
6. Did I engage with the audience or did I stay hidden behind the lectern?
7. What could I do next time to make it better? What would I add or change next time to make it more effective?
8. What were the parts of the discussion that excited me the most?
9. What seemed to move/touch/grab the audience the most?
10. Did this speech change my thinking about myself as a speaker? How or how not?
11. What went well?
12. What went wrong?
13. What would I do differently next time?

When you perform at your best, especially in front of a supportive audience, those who follow you will also up their game and perform at a higher level. The next time you take the stage, don't forget that you will have many fans in the audience, even those you just met, or for whom you present a favorable first impression -- they are still hoping for you to succeed.

14

Wrapping the Gift With a Bow

"Start with the end in mind."
– Stephen M.R. Covey

Many people have asked me how I got started as an author and how I wrote my initial 300-page textbook for my 6-week and 4-day courses. I took Stephen Covey's advice from the quote above and began with the end in mind. I wanted a stand-alone learning opportunity for both my in-class and coaching clients, but also something that a self-learner could use as a "student from afar." The textbook far exceeded my clients' expectations and I'm happy to be able to release this version into the world. I look forward to hearing how far my knowledge travels!

Let's return to the main point of my book: "What's your #1 goal of any presentation? Answer: To be remembered." Like the late great Mr. Covey says… *"start with the end in mind."* As you complete your speech outline in Appendix A, ask yourself if you're using all the tools and strategies that I've shared. All of this is provided to give you the best chance of having what you share in your speeches remembered, cherished, and utilized.

How will you know that you have succeeded in achieving the goal of being remembered?

One day in the future, a week, a month, or years later, you will run into one of your audience members, somewhere unexpectedly. They should be able to tell you not only what your topic was, but your three main points as well. That's powerful -- you will not believe how awesome you'll feel when you realize that you did such a great job on that presentation waaaaaaay back when!

When that happens, I'd love for you to email me and share that story. It fills my heart to hear that my gift is being shared around the world and helping in some small way to change the lives of others.

Now turning to my concluding advice, I always stress the importance of using a proper conclusion to any presentation. I call this final step -- "wrapping it with a bow." Returning to the theme of this book, I give this gift of my knowledge and expertise to you with the hopes that it will help to lessen your presentation anxiety. Now, I will add the "bow."

It is my deepest wish that each speech you present from now until the day you leave this earth will be much easier to craft, present, and learn from; and that you will improve each and every time you're called on to share your wisdom. I am optimistic that each time you pick up this book to re-read my tips and strategies, you will develop an amazing speaking persona. One day, you will experience a "breakthrough presentation" where you will be reborn as a confident speaker.

When you do have your breakthrough, I'd love to see you putting my strategies into action! I'd be honoured if you'd share a video or YouTube link with me when you feel that it's all come together for you and you've been able to break through your inhibitions and to grow as a speaker. You will know when a breakthrough happens; I have seen it occur many times in my 6-week and 4-day classes for who trust in the process of "growing the distance." Becoming an amazing speaker is not an overnight occurrence, but I know that with practice and the pursuit of continuous improvement, you will achieve your dreams. It is truly awe inspiring to feel everything click in that moment -- I'd love to share that with you.

Public speaking is like any muscle in your body, and we all know what happens when we stop going to the gym or slack off on our athletic pursuits… we lose muscle tone. The same is true of the techniques in this book. You will need to keep practicing these techniques every month and year throughout your life so that you stay sharp and "in shape." I encourage you to accept any and all speaking opportunities and to consider joining an organization such as Toastmasters International, or starting your own informal speaking club. It would be the ultimate compliment if you used my book for such a club, or even if you wished to use this information in your non-fiction book club readings. I'd be happy to supply additional feedback and support.

If, after finishing this book, you desire additional coaching or assistance on obtaining your breakthrough quicker, or if you should ever feel stuck when asked to present, please feel free to reach out to me. I provide one-on-one speech crafting and speech-delivery coaching services via Skype and FaceTime, and I can tailor a variety of services to suit your individual requirements. We all require a bit of fine-tuning on our speaking persona, sometimes, and I'd be happy to help you.

Special Offer

As mentioned at the beginning of this book, I'd love to reward your efforts to craft an amazing presentation with 50% off a one-hour coaching session (via Skype or FaceTime) for me to view and comment on your speaking persona. You can choose to run through your polished presentation live, or to provide a video to me (via Youtube), which I'd be happy to evaluate using the criteria in Chapter 13 of this book.

I love seeing my recommended strategies in action!

Hope to hear from you soon.

Appendix A: G2G Secret Formula Speech Crafting Outline

Part A - Introduction (10% of your speech)
Tell them what you are going to tell them

What is the focus of your speech (TOPIC)? What would be a good TITLE for your speech?

Persuasive: What is your stance on the topic?

What's in it for me (W.I.I.F.M.)? Why should the audience care about your chosen topic? Why should this be important to them NOW?

Persuasive: Why should the audience change their perception of the topic? Are there any deadlines or reasons that they should take action immediately?

Persuasive: What is your destination? Where do you want the audience to end up?

What are your three main points?

Persuasive: What are the three most logical steps to convince them of your opinion from your brainstorming exercises? NOTE: #3 could be most important point! Use it last this time, IF you time it well.

1. _____

2. _____

3. _____

Establish your credibility - why are you an "expert" on this subject? How much experience do you have with this subject?

The Hook: What research question could you open your speech with to learn more about your audience?

Persuasive: What do you not yet know about your listeners?

PART B - BODY (80% of your speech)
Tell them

1. What is your most important main point to this audience?

    Sub/Supporting Point 1A:

    _____

    Sub/Supporting Point 1B:

    _____

    Sub/Supporting Point 1C:

    _____

2. What is your next most important main point?

    Sub/Supporting Point 2A:

    _____

    Sub/Supporting Point 2B:

    _____

    Sub/Supporting Point 2C:

    _____

3. What is your least important main point?

> Sub/Supporting Point 3A:
>
> _____
>
> Sub/Supporting Point 3B:
>
> _____
>
> Sub/Supporting Point 3C:
>
> _____

PART C - CONCLUSION (10% of your speech)
Tell them what you told them

What were your three main points?

NOTE: Do not add any additional points, which will only confuse the audience!

1. _____

2. _____

3. _____

Why should this be important to the audience NOW?

> *Persuasive*: What can the audience do NOW to get started? What is the next step? Give them an action item i.e. phone number, where to buy a product, who to write to, what to do when they get home or tomorrow morning first thing.

What is the last impression that you will leave with the audience – a quotation, statistic/fact, action step or tip?

Appendix B: General Speech Outline Worksheet

Introduction

10% of your allotted time
Total Minutes:

TOPIC:	
W.I.I.F.M.:	
THREE POINTS:	1.
	2.
	3.
CREDIBILITY:	
CONVERSATION STARTER:	

Body

80% of your allotted time
Total Minutes:

Main Point 1 (most important) Total Minutes:	
1A.	
1B.	
1C.	
CONVERSATION OPPORTUNITY:	

Main Point 2 (next important) - Total Minutes:	
2A.	
2B.	
2C.	
CONVERSATION OPPORTUNITY:	
Main Point 3 (least important) - Total Minutes:	
3A.	
3B.	
3C.	
CONVERSATION OPPORTUNITY:	

Conclusion

10% of your allotted time
Total Minutes:

THREE POINTS:	1.
	2.
	3.
IMPORTANCE:	
ZINGER:	

Appendix C: Speaking Math Calculations

A proper balance of points when presenting is important. You neither want to jam everything into the first of your three points so the backend of your speech feels light, nor do you want to backload your presentation and rush through your final points.

If you use my Speaking Math calculation below I promise that you will harmonious balance your presentation and each of the areas and points effectively. Keep the one-page outline handy while you review this and jot each of the calculations in to your outline as you compute them.

1. Total time allotted to you, excluding question and answer period: _____ minutes

   Note: If you're given an hour or more, change it to minutes by multiplying by 60)

2. Multiply total time by 0.1 (10%): _____ minutes

   This is roughly the maximum time you should spend on your Introduction. Be careful to minimize how long you spend at the beginning of your speech, as you will be stealing minutes later from your limited time.

3. Multiply your total time by 0.8 (80%): _____ minutes

   This is the maximum time you actually have to talk and expand on the Body of your presentation

4. Multiply total time by 0.1 (10%): _____ minutes

   This is roughly the maximum time you should spend on your Conclusion, and it is sacred time that you need to save in order to effectively wrap up your presentation.

5. Take the number of minutes from #3 and divide that by 3: _____ minutes

This is how much time you will have to speak about and expand on each of your three main points.

6. Take the number of minutes from #5 and divide that by 3 again: _____ minutes

For each main point (3 in total) you will up to 3 sub-points (sometimes only two, and at the most you may have 4 sub-points). This calculation will show you how much time you have to chat about each sub point.

Use my Speaking Math calculations to keep you on time and on-schedule so that you get to effectively share everything that you planned. This exercise can be a real eye-opener to help you cut down your presentation into just what you absolutely need to share given your time constraints.

For example, a 1-hour / 60-minute speech should have a 6-minute introduction, 48-minute body with 16 minutes per main point and about 5 minutes per sub point, and a 6-minute conclusion.

Appendix D: Questions for Future Speaking Engagements

Before accepting an invitation to speak, you should always ask these questions of the organizer as the answers will assist you in your preparation and avoid any uncomfortable surprises.

1. Name of your on-site contact person and/or audio-visual person, if applicable.
2. What is the purpose of the meeting?
3. Is this a formal or informal gathering?
4. Is your talk the main attraction i.e. keynote, or will others be presenting?
5. What is the full agenda for the event?
6. At what time of day will you be speaking?
7. How long are you expected to present in total?
8. Does that time include a question period?
9. What are the other speakers presenting?
10. Where exactly will you be speaking?
11. How will the room be setup?
12. What equipment is available for audio/visual purposes?
13. What is the size of the audience?
14. Is the audience required to attend?
15. Are they paying to attend? If so, how much?
16. How much does your audience know about your topic?
17. Will the audience be served alcohol?
18. Will they be stationary or are some audience members drifting in and out of the room?
19. What other speakers have they heard on the subject and how have they responded?
20. Can you change or adjust the chosen topic?

Acknowledgements

I would like to thank all of my clients over the years who have made the content of this book a possibility. I have had the pleasure of training and coaching hundreds of people how to cure their fear of public speaking, and they have in turn taught me and fed my passion for education. Thank You!

To my darling husband, Jeff, who is blessed with the patience of an angel. Thank you for being the first editor of my work, and my #1 proofreader in all things. I so appreciate you and our love. Thank You!

To my #1 fan and the woman who I have been blessed to know since Kindergarten. Thank you Corinne (Stamm) Brownlee for coming back into my life just a couple years ago. I am so very grateful that the angels brought us back together and that you have been my biggest cheerleader over the past 18 months when I spoke my crazy dream to complete the first draft of this book in just 30 days. You have been a truly incredible editor and such a great support. A million times – thank you. I could not have done this without you! Thank You!

Thank you Hadass Eviatar, my "Professional Enabler" for all the confidence, support, and thought provoking input and edits. I appreciate the time you took as my third editor to review and find all the things that we missed. Thank You!

To my fantastic interior design friend, Charmaine Lyons, who is also the only past student of mine to have edited the book. I appreciate all the support you gave to this project. Thanks for taking the time to read my binder full of pages. I am always so thankful of your insight and special flare. Thank You!

To Angela Mondor, my Geeky Girl, right-hand I.T., social media guru, who has always been there to help me with software and website challenges – you really know your stuff and can definitely translate it into non-geek-speak. I appreciate your assistance in the editing process, and I appreciate all of your support for my new website and blog on the subject of public speaking. I know I could never struggle through all my online challenges without your constant support. Thank you for always being there when I needed to hear a voice on the end of the phone. Thank You!

To all the members of Anna's Advisory (Secret) Group on Facebook. Thank You! Your support throughout the past two years was incredible, especially while I was writing my first 50,000 words for this book by staying committed to the process to finish it in just one month. February 28th, 2013 was a great month in an attempt to attain my daily target of words on the page, and I appreciate all of your support.

My initial inspiration to write this book came from a fellow author, Barb Kobylak Chabai (aka Barb Kellyn) author of The Company She Keeps and Morning Man. As a local Winnipeg author, she showed me the "golden pathway" and shared with me how she wrote both her books in just one month each using Chris Baty's techniques. Thank You!

The golden pathway for a first time author comes in the form of Chris Baty's book No Plot No Problem, and his amazing NaNoWriMo project. In his book, Chris teaches how to write a 50,000-word book in just 30 days. So, I'm paying it forward and hope to inspire future authors to get their book out of their head and on paper, to make that big checkmark on their Bucket List and "Get 'er Done!" For more information pick up Chris Baty's eBook or book, join his Facebook Page and sign up on his website www.NaNoWriMo.org to join the National Novel Writing Month in November (also April and July now) to write your first book.

Finally, a huge thank you to my business mentor, and writing angel, Barbara Bowes, who is an inspiration to many businesswomen (and men) in and around Winnipeg. I so appreciated your editing assistance on this project, not once, but twice. I cannot thank you enough for your mentorship, and how much it has meant to me over the past year. Thank you for you encouragement and support.

I have tears in my eyes as I write this last page of the book and count all my blessings and all the angels who have made my first attempt at writing a book possible. I can't believe that I am writing this Acknowledgements page sitting here with my first book (of many I hope) completed and ready to head off to a publisher. Whew! I truly never thought that I could do this, and I know that I could not have done it without the assistance of all these great people.

I never believed that I could write a book. But, looking back to the goals I wrote for myself in 1999, I realized that I've wanted to write this book for a long time. I never could have done it without everyone's support each and every day of this process. Thank You!

About the Author

Over the past 15 years, Anna's compassionate and confidence-boosting methods and unique teaching techniques have helped hundreds of clients from all walks of life to become confident speakers and presenters.

As the founder of GoodToGreat Public Speaking Training, Anna delivers her six-week and four-day courses, Giving the Gift of Public Speaking to clients throughout Canada, and she hopes to hear from others requiring this knowledge across the United States and around the world. To facilitate training at a distance, there is also the choice of one-on-one coaching and critical speech feedback via Skype/FaceTime or Youtube.

In addition, Anna has authored "Presenting Fearlessly: A Guide to Slaying the 37 Most Common Presentation Anxieties," and was a contributing author to "The Coaching Gurus" anthology. She also has posted almost 100 helpful tips at: www.goodtogreatps.com/blog

Anna is the proud mother of two "fur-kids," Mitzie and Toby, and wife to the best editor a woman can have, her husband, Jeff. Having lived all across Western Canada over the past 25 years, Anna and Jeff have currently settled in Victoria to enjoy a different lifestyle than they had in Winnipeg.

Anna is a serious foodie and loves being involved in a variety of local projects and getting out to talk to chefs and producers. She's shared many a great meal and enjoys learning new culinary tricks in the kitchen when she has the time to cook – you can check out some of her endeavours on her casual food blog at LunchFor1.com.

It's not all work and no play for Anna, as she a bit of a social butterfly too. She also loves to nap, catch up with friends and family on social media or maybe over a glass of red wine or cup of tea, and host friendly dinner parties with other foodies.

Anna especially loves to hear from her past clients about how their newfound gifts in the public speaking realm have helped them to advanced in their careers and lives. So please feel free to reach out to her at Anna@GoodToGreatPS.com with your stories and comments.

Good To GREAT
public speaking training

Anna Coleshaw-Echols
Chief Fear Slayer

Contact Information

GoodToGreat Public Speaking Training

250-217-1811

Anna@GoodToGreatPS.com

www.GoodToGreatPS.com

LINKEDIN.COM/IN/AECHOLS

FACEBOOK.COM/GOODTOGREATPS

TWITTER.COM/GOODTOGREATPS

PINTEREST.COM/GOODTOGREATPS